THE GATHERING

When The Rapture
Really Happens

WAYNE DESLATTES

CHARISM PRESS PUBLISHING

ISBN 979-8-9854818-0-8
U.S. Copyright Office Reg.# TXu 2 - 296 - 868
Library of Congress Control Number: 2022900025
Printed in The United States of America. 2022

CONTENTS

ACKNOWLEDGMENTS

I give credit to the Lord Who taught me, and gave me the insight and motivation to write this, and Who tells me everything is possible.

PREFACE

I came to write this book not with the purpose of refuting a prejudged stance, but rather by the questions and insights about it that have percolated in my heart and mind for over twenty years as I saw discrepancies in what I was taught. I later read the book, *Rapture Under Attack,* which was meant to fortify the pre-tribulation rapture position, hence the name. However after reading it, I found it firmed the inaccuracy of this long-held position even more for me. So, I sought to uncover what the Bible said for myself without the influence of men's views and opinions. Gathering a lot of opinions to support a view is easy to do. This doesn't necessarily make the stance true and determinate because many think the same way. It only shows one has found more people who believe the same thing. The voice of the many isn't right if God's Word conflicts with it. I believe that some authors who wrote about the rapture had a position they wanted to prove first. I studied for scripture to reveal itself and thereby set my view. My goal is to lead readers along the sequential path of scriptural clues to an eventual conclusion, not basing it upon what this man thinks or what that theologian thought or what twenty other authors wrote to support what one believes. Scripture and Jesus's words are good enough and strong enough. This book is meant to answer long debated questions about the raptures placement in Revelations and to increase the reader's hope and faith in the strength of God's promises going forward.

It is the glory of God to conceal things, but it is the glory of kings to search things out. Proverbs 25:2 ESV

INTRODUCTION

Is another book on the rapture needed? Yes, I think it really is. With the outbreak of the COVID 19 virus, civil unrest and global societal changes, the world is accelerating towards Christ's return. Old and young Christians alike have a renewed interest—and with good reason. His return is nearer than ever and the Church needs to wake up, watch and get ready for Him! Various stances about the rapture, and its position to the tribulation, have been debated over many years. Large swaths of mainline Christians and Christian denominations believe a certain proposed and assumed rapture-tribulation position that's never been scripturally proven. This book will now lay the uncertainty to rest.

To say Christ's return will be a major event is a gross understatement. It is the main event since His cross and empty tomb. It's what Christians everywhere look forward to. I don't think He wants people to be ignorant of nor confused about it. With fresh insights in scripture from the Lord, we can pinpoint the placement of the rapture in Revelation. When does the rapture *really* happen in Revelation? Where exactly does it occur in position to the tribulation? How will it happen? Will Christians live on earth during the tribulation period? These questions and more will be answered, and readers will see what the Bible actually says about the pre-trib rapture view — it will surprise you. My desire is this book helps people better understand Revelation and prophetic scripture, to shine light on what the Bible more fully teaches about the rapture with sequence and paradox, that it encourages faith and hope in God's promises, and re-invigorates a new excitement about Jesus's return, as it has me.

PART ONE

CHAPTER ONE

WHERE WE BEGIN

W ho doesn't want to know the future? There is much expectation about the future and Christ's return by Christians since the onset of the *Covid-19* virus with all its collateral effects. Yet for some, it's not on their radar at all. One of the more mysterious topics in the Bible, and one of the most debated, is the event we call the rapture and when it will occur. I remember from the late 70's into the 80's, there was a lot of preaching about Jesus' return. There was so much speculation about its nearness that I remember thinking I wouldn't live past 1984 because Jesus would have come by then. I don't know why I thought that was the year. Maybe it had something to do with George Orwell's book, *1984*.[1]

Did any of you see the 1972 movie, *A Thief in The Night*?[2] It was semi-popular in Christian subculture and the forerunner to the 2000 *Left Behind* movie with actor Kirk Cameron.[3] The movie soundtrack was by Larry Norman, "I Wish We'd All Been Ready" which you can listen to on YouTube.[4]

From the movie outset, the rapture occurs then depicts life for a handful of people who remained struggling through the course of the Tribulation Period, unwilling to take 'the mark'. I sat in a pew near the back of the church with my youth group friends as our congregation watched the film. It was a good movie and it made an impact, but to be frank, it really unnerved me. For weeks I was afraid I would be left behind in some tribulated-dystopian city with others who somehow "missed the elevator," covertly maneuvering daily from a modern American Gestapo.

As a young person, I listened to many invited guest preachers and evangelists at my church who shared prophecies and revelations they believed to come from God and their reading of Revelation. The messages captivated me but also caused me to fear. Later, at nineteen years of age, I received Christ as my Savior. Since that happened, I don't fear the future like I did. Still for me, there was this unknown hiddenness surrounding the rapture, something that didn't fit.

In the mid to late 90s, millions of people read Tim LaHaye and Jerry Jenkins' compilation called the *Left Behind* series. The *Left Behind* series is known as Christian prophetic fiction. This means it's fiction based on future prophetic events. Although the rapture event is a true, scriptural future event, how the story line would play out with the characters and events is their conjecture. It sold millions of copies.

Selling millions of copies proves it must be accurate, right? Popularity and high-volume sales don't make a position accurate. I mention this since many people are familiar with the series, but we will look at this perspective more closely later—trust me, you don't want to miss it. I'm going to show you what the Bible really reveals about the rapture.

PROPHETIC SCRIPTURE AND THE BOOK OF REVELATION

For anyone reading, who is unfamiliar with the Bible, I'd like to lay a base for understanding it. There are sixty-six books comprised in the Bible, varying in type. Some are purely historical record while others are proverb, prose, song, poetry, prophecy and doctrine. Within the New Testament, there are personal letters written to believers and corporate letters written to churches, historical records of Jesus' life and teachings, and prophecy.

If we are going to read Scripture, we need to know the difference between inspiration and illumination. God inspired the biblical authors what to write. Second Timothy 3: 16 states all biblical scripture was inspired (God-breathed) by the Holy Spirit. Second Peter 1:20 – 21 says, "Above all, you must understand that no prophecy of scripture came about by the prophet's own interpretation of things. For prophecy never had its origin in the human will, but prophets, though human, spoke from God as they were carried along by the Holy Spirit" (NIV). That's inspiration. What the Holy Spirit does with inspired Scripture is illuminate our minds so we can understand it. Anything the Holy Spirit teaches us from it is illumination. There is no more inspiration to be added to the Bible, only illumination to understand it. By this basis, it'll be understood what I mean when I say *what this person said is inspired versus what that person said is opinion.*

Prophecy makes up nearly one-third of the body of

biblical Scripture. There are hundreds of recorded prophecies spoken by God to men and women and given to writers, which became scripture to pass along to future generations. Psalms is one of the largest prophetic books formed from prose, poetry and songs, and written largely by the prophet David, also known as King David. Prophets wrote the last half of the Old Testament books, which are prophetic to the historical recorded events of the day, and additionally prophetic about Jesus' life, the Church, and the end times and last days.

To understand prophecy better, its beneficial to realize some prophecy protocols like prophetic delay, the use of signs, layered prophecy and paradox; I'll explain a few.

One rule is about time and timing. Time and timing in a prophecy can be puzzling. Signs usually signal something is coming but not present yet. Another fundamental of prophecy is that fulfillment may not be simultaneous with the sign's appearance. We might call this prophetic delay because the *something* comes *after* but still near the sign. Next, another rule to remember is that prophecies can be layered with more than one application in time. We often think in a monochromatic-linear way while God is thinking and working in dimensions and layers. The Psalms 8 and Revelation 12 are examples of layered prophecy. Also, a sign can exist but not be recognized. For example, the predicted star signifying Jesus' birth existed for a long time with only the few Magi recognizing it.

Comparing prophecies is another protocol. In the Old Testament, prophets congregated together and mentored younger, up-incoming prophets. They would share and compare prophetic words to validate their messages from the Lord and to gain fuller meanings. First Corinthians 13:9

states 'we know in part and we prophesy in part'. This means if three of us have a prophetic word for someone, that person will gain the fuller picture of what God is communicating when the *words* are compared and added together. Prophecies and prophetic words are understood better and validated by a company of prophets as each one brings the prophetic part they received, then puts them together to reinforce the meaning more fully. Prophetic scriptures are more fully understood when compared to other prophetic scripture about the same matter. I'll bring some of these guidelines for understanding prophecy to our attention later when applicable.

REVELATION

The book of Revelation is apocalyptic literature. It is a book we will spend time in. People sometimes confuse the term *apocalypse* with *catastrophe*: they're not the same. Catastrophes can be a part of an apocalypse but may not be. Apocalypse in the old Greek language literally means *from cover* or an uncovering, hence a revealing or revelation. This literary form was common in Apostle John's day. Religiously, apocalypse refers to something very important which was hidden. Because such a large segment of Scripture is prophetic, it shouldn't be unusual to discuss Bible prophecy and prophetic messages today. Unfortunately, many Christians rarely read this genre of biblical literature. Sometimes, people don't like to hear messages from Revelation because the catastrophes it foretells frightens them. The passages can also be difficult to understand. While reading and studying Revelation, pay attention to the beginnings and endings of the visions and scenes the apostle John recorded.

Remember, there is an order in which they were shown to John by which he recorded them but they may not be completely chronological in earthly order and may overlap and layer. I hope this book changes any unappetizing prospect towards Revelation and solidifies more faith in God's promises for readers.

Once Jesus saved me, my view of Revelation changed. Before my salvation experience, reading Revelation unsettled me. But then I was excited to know when He is coming back. I understand better now than I did then that Revelation is primarily about the revealing (uncovering) of Jesus and His return, culminating the redemption of saints and the eviction of evil from the world. The gospels do a good job providing a close view of what Jesus was like as the humble servant, Son of Man, but Revelation provides the best description of what Jesus is like in His glory. If you want to know Jesus better and learn what He is really like past the human form—read Revelation devotionally. He is supremely powerful, ultimately sovereign and totally in control of everything in the last days. The more I read it I see how incomparably more powerful He is than the powers of Darkness. He laughs at their attempt (Ps. 2:1–5). By the way, Revelation is the only book stating for whomever reads it, they will be blessed (Rev.1:3). So, I encourage you—read it and be blessed!

With this baseline understanding of the Bible and prophecy, let's move forward to understand what we have been taught.

CHAPTER TWO

ON VIEWS AND OPINIONS

W hat you do or don't believe about His return and the rapture won't affect the manner or timing in which He will come back. I find many people are comfortable living their lives day after day, focusing on the present with only anticipation of family and retirement. And if future events hold something unpleasant—forget about it. If the last days aren't a neat little pain-free package, people don't want to know. It is no different today as it has been down through centuries. People, even Christians, don't want to hear a prophetic message threatening their good time. I'm not saying this book will endanger anyone's good time; however, I will not say the Bible says something it doesn't. Jesus particularly said, at the end of Revelation 22:18–19, that we should be careful to not add or take away from that book, so I've taken care to not do so. I won't interpret the Bible because there is no need for me to, but I will explain parts of it. Some prophecies loaded with symbols can be challenging to understand. Most of the rapture passages I have quoted are pretty clear-cut with little symbolism; we'll get through them just fine.

There is a pervasive belief today that the rapture will occur before the Tribulation Period begins with Jesus keeping believers from experiencing any of the seven-year trial called the Tribulation. It sounds good and makes for a nice ending. But is it true? We'll explore it. I think this view creates a cavalier attitude in some believers regarding how they live. We believe that because God is good (and He absolutely is) He won't make us experience any of the tribulation courses. Because of this belief, most have hardly studied it because it won't affect us—or so we think. Perhaps our faith is in the *Left Behind* stories, or that someone told us we will be gone, that no difficulty will come our way and God will package our earthly Christian experience neatly with a bow. Like a proverbial ostrich burying its head in the sand, the inward thought may be *if I don't hear it, I don't have to think about it. Ignoring it will make it go away. I like this preacher's take on it better. I'll believe that.*

Question: Whether you think you might live during the Tribulation or not, wouldn't it interest you to know more about it? After all, God included plenty of passages about it in the Old and New Testament. What would change in your ten, twenty, or thirty-year plan? You would want to be prepared as well as you could, if possible, right? Because some Christians do not believe they will undergo this, they are hardly interested. If you think, *As long as my family and I are saved, I'm happy and I'm done. We won't be here, so* . . . you might be one of the disinterested. Whether we believe it is pre, mid or post, we should watch for Jesus' return and read and re-read Revelation.

Approaching this topic, preachers and academics try to

prove their view instead of letting Scripture set it. As ministers, we do our best to study Scripture objectively, but sometimes we inadvertently bend it by our own opinion.

Volumes on this subject are full of assumptions. Often, these books are subjective and skewed by the stance the authors believe in and want to prove first, instead of letting God's Word lead them. Specially, I didn't want to do that. Why fill a book with the sentiments of men and women whose words are not Holy Spirit-inspired like Jesus and Paul's words? I didn't come at this with a doctrine I wanted to prove or a reputation to protect. Nor am I running for some religious-political position. In the text of Scripture, it will show what it shows, and I will do my best to keep explanations simple and understandable. If you can, put aside pre-conceived ideas; let God's Word lead what you think. Ask the Holy Spirit to illuminate your understanding. One question I repeatedly asked throughout this study is *where do we see the details given by Jesus and Paul occurring in Revelation?*

Where the markers lie in the book of Revelation is more important than proving one's view. In fact, where they lie should set our view. A biased slant may not always lead to truth, but the truth is where we want to go. Let's allow scripture to change what we think, even if it differs from what we previously thought. This is a purpose of Scripture; to change what we think, to renew our minds with truth, to make us more like Christ, and to lead us into fresh experiences with Jesus Himself.

WHAT WE ARE TAUGHT

Does it seem nervy to say definitively whether the rapture is pre, mid, or post-trib? I don't think so. Many have done so for centuries. I say let Scripture speak truly . . . and it will as we let it form what we believe. People say *Well, people have speculated this view for decades, but I don't think anyone really knows.* Yes, people have speculated for decades, even hundreds of years. But to say no one knows nor can know— I don't agree. The answer has been there all along. Many believers have denied what the Bible says about the rapture's position relevant to the Tribulation. For a long time, I didn't see it. I couldn't because I didn't believe it. For years, my teachers taught me "this is when it happens." I believed them because all those around me were taught the same. *Well, doesn't that make you think what they taught you is true, since they believed it?* you might ask. Well, I did, but now, no.

To illustrate belief change, as a teenager, I was taught dancing was wrong to do. As a young adult, I studied it for myself and discovered no such thing in the Bible. To the contrary, it is sanctioned as an expression of worship. Granted, people can misuse dance just like they can song or money, but that doesn't mean we should avoid them entirely. All along, it was a subjective, unscriptural stance.

Once you're taught something is a certain way for so long by persons you admire and respect, it's difficult to concede they were *off base* on a matter. It doesn't make them bad people or reduce their worth, respect or honor. You know, I don't see any denominations having all their beliefs and practices wholly align with Scripture yet. I believe every Christian denomination has received a measure of God's truth, but I don't see any having it all together correct yet.

Regarding the rapture and Christ's return, I discovered some tenets taught to me were incongruent with Scripture and conflicted with simple reading comprehension. It's like when someone tells you for years "this verse says this". You never question it but accept what he or she says as true. Whenever you objectively read the verse, you might think, *Wait, now where in this verse does it really say what they told me it said? How did they get that idea when there are no words in the sentence to communicate such?* That's what I mean. It's problematic when a person quotes prophetic Scriptures that say nothing pertaining to the rapture, and then they read more into the verses than what is there. Many verses are misread, stretched, and colored this way through a prescribed lens of belief and a pre-decided view. Revelation 4:1–2 is one instance (Just wait. There's a whole chapter on these verses). But we are going to look with impartial eyes and see what the Bible says.

I didn't approach this subject desiring to dispel any position. I wanted to let Scripture say what it says. The result I found surprised me. The clues God revealed to me confirm my thoughts and heighten my awareness. After writing this book, I can truly say I anticipate His coming more than ever. My hope is people will see clearly what Scripture says and believe it because Jesus' return is nearer than ever and we need to be primed. It is something we need to know, and I conclude He wants us to know. As believers in Christ, it's what we've been waiting for. Let's get started.

CHAPTER THREE

WHAT IS THE RAPTURE?

W hat is the rapture? What does it have to do with Jesus' return? Rapture is a word not found in the Bible, just like we don't find the term *trinity*. The fact the word isn't present doesn't mean the concept, the illustration and the teaching of it aren't present in the Bible. They are found in both the Old and New Testament.

Some Old Testament verses that hint to the rapture are Ezekiel 34:12, where the LORD gathers His sheep; in Zephaniah 2:3b where the LORD hides His people; and Ezekiel 37:12–14 infers the future rapture by the raising of His people from their graves, and Isaiah 60:8 refers to those "who fly like a cloud, like doves . . .".

It is described in many New Testament passages which we will examine, but what is it? It's not heaven or paradise. It's an event: a snatching up, or a gathering up of the righteous from the Earth. The rapture is the 'blink of an eye' miracle wherein Jesus Christ returns to gather all His people who repented and professed faith in Him, including the bodies of dead believers, to meet Him in the clouds and air, and forever be with Him in Heaven. Believers will arrive in Heaven eventually, but initially the Bible says we'll meet Him in the clouds and air, not Heaven.

THE ORIGINATION OF 'RAPTURE'

The term 'rapture' was believed to be anglicized by C. I. Schofield, who coined it in his self-published Bible version, from the Latin words *raeptius,* and *rapiemur* from the Latin Vulgate, which are similar equivalents for the Greek word *harpazo* used in the First Thessalonians 4:17 passage.[1] Harpazo means 'caught up' and the Latin means more closely 'grabbed or taken away'. It is also the same word used in Acts 8:39 describing Philip's teleportation to Azotus, and by Apostle Paul in Second Corinthians 12:2 and verse 4 (describing his experience), and in Revelations 12:5. 'Caught up' and 'taken away' are used in many newer Bible translations. Grammatically, changing a verb to a noun is called nouning, or nominalization. It isn't incorrect to do.[2, 3] 'Rapture' is the Latin verb derivative made into a noun to assign the act to this specific event. It caught on through the years and people have been using it ever since.

FORMS OF CATCHING UP

The thought of being raptured or caught up may seem strange (and it is) is because we haven't seen it happening. There are many instances in the Bible where the Lord takes a person 'in the spirit' (or by their spirit) to other places to show or teach them something; like the prophets Ezekiel and Isaiah, and Apostle John to name a few. But these aren't a 'bodily taking' as with the rapture. God's taking of persons from this world is not new, really. Here are some examples. The Bible records Enoch never died but was translated, or taken (Gen. 5:24, Heb. 11:5). Elijah never died but was taken up in a whirlwind on a fiery chariot (2 Kings 2:1, 11). How about that for an out of this world exit? Philip had just finished leading an Ethiopian eunuch to faith when the Lord snatched him up from Gaza and placed him thirty-two miles away in Azotus. Jesus ascended as the disciples stood there astonished (Acts 1:9–10). Those disciples who saw him ascend were first New Testament eyewitnesses to a person taken up all the way out of sight in the sky. All these are examples of persons who left this world alive, though each exit differed. Notwithstanding, the disciples who saw Jesus ascend had a better grasp than any how the rapture might appear. When these disciples testified to what they saw, you can imagine people would believe them and want to join their group. Revelation 11:12 states the two specific prophets wreaking havoc on the earth will ascend to heaven.

God has caught up and taken out of this world, persons He wanted to move or bring home specially. He could choose a hundred ways to take us, but He has chosen this as the way we get to exit the world. I know we're going to love it.

Where is the rapture really mentioned in Revelation? Can we show it without ambiguous verses and suppositions? Is it before, during, or after the Tribulation? What did Jesus say about it? Do we know how we shall be taken up? The answers to these are coming.

CHAPTER FOUR

WHAT JESUS SAID

Whenever I have an ethical or moral question, for which I don't already know the answer, I try to find what Jesus said about it. If we should believe what any historical biblical character has to say about something, we ought to believe what Jesus Christ said, don't you think? After all, He is the Faithful Witness (Rev. 1:5). This means He has been and is faithful in His witness of the truth and will not lie about anything; the Father and His purposes, His commands, and His character. He was and still is the unwavering Witness of the Father and all that is godly. Because He is the truth, it means He is the Source of all truth, which begins in and originates from Him.

When we want to know the truth about something, we look to what Jesus said. So then, if we believe Jesus is sinless, has never lied and always told the truth, then we should believe the red letters in our Bibles—His recorded words. Right? If we won't receive Jesus' words as true, then how can we position the words of any other historical or present personality as more reliable? We must believe and accept His words as infallible truth.

For this chapter, I will use the plain, non-figurative words Jesus used in describing the last days and His return, not parables. Whatever Jesus said, He won't contradict Himself in any metaphor He used. Any metaphorical understanding which we have should not contradict what Jesus said literally and plainly. Therefore, whatever He said about His return and our gathering should be final. Whoever will not accept Jesus' words as final will have difficulty accepting what is true and real. Let us remember Jesus' admonition to not add to nor take away from the words of the book, particularly Revelation (22:18–19).

The Lord tells His plans before executing them. Amos 3:7 says, "For the LORD God does nothing without revealing his secret to his servants the prophets." Jesus told the disciples in John 15:15, that He no longer called them servants but friends. Why? Masters don't disclose details to slaves. They don't share inner thoughts and plans with them. One simply commands them to *do this or that.* People divulge plans, details, and desires in intimately growing relationships. With friends, you want to disclose your intentions. You want them to know more information, and personally more, you. Jesus shared with them the program because He wanted them to know, otherwise He wouldn't have told His disciples the program. Since they knew, we know. God speaks today because He wants us to know His plans for us. He is pleased to tell His people what He is up to just like He was pleased to tell Jesus.

TERMS OF SEQUENCE

The largest passages spoken by Jesus about the end times and His return are recorded in the Gospel books by Matthew chapter 24, Mark chapter 13 and Luke chapter 21. His disciples asked when His return would be and what it would be like. He told them. *But wait . . . no one knows the day or the hour!* You are correct. No one knows the day or hour. Jesus said no one knew the hour or day but only His Father in Heaven (Matt. 24:36). However, He foretold by listing signs and events, the sequence by which they would occur, and so, for what to watch.

If I say I'm going away but I'm coming back—I don't know exactly when I am returning, but plants will bud and flower, then fruits and vegetables will produce, and then later be harvested. People will feast with their families on turkey and dressing, ham and more. Then the weather will get colder, and gifts will encircle decorated trees. Then, after this, I will come immediately. By my description listing sequential events, you could deduce I would return promptly after the Christmas holiday without me ever mentioning an hour, a day, or year. The events I listed occur every year, so narrowing down what specific year could be a problem. This is what Jesus did; He used terms of sequence.

There are accounts in three gospels recording Jesus' prediction about His return and our rapture. All three accounts are reliable. Since they are Jesus' words, we know they are true. Since each gospel record agrees with the others, we know they are accurate. Matthew 24 will be our key text. The other two, I will reference later. Let's begin, starting in the passage Matthew 24:1–31 where Jesus prophesied about the Temple.

> Jesus left the temple and was walking away when his disciples came up to him to call his attention to its buildings. "Do you see all these things?" he asked. "Truly I tell you, not one stone here will be left on another; every one will be thrown down." As Jesus was sitting on the Mount of Olives, the disciples came to him privately. "Tell us," they said, "when will this happen, and what will be the sign of your coming and of the end of the age? (Matt. 24:1–3 [NIV])

The disciples obviously connected the destruction of the Temple with His return and the last days, so they curiously asked. In Matthew 24:4–20, He described and designated events that would occur as the timing would draw nearer; many counterfeit Christs will appear, there will be wars and rumors of wars, famines, pestilences, earthquakes, etc. These are the beginning of miseries. Believers will be hated and persecuted and "then shall many be offended, and shall betray one another, and shall hate one another." This sounds like today's culture, doesn't it . . . people offending and being offended, shaming and forcing them to cower to various 'woke agendas'? Suffering and persecution can, but may not always, surface as physical harm and death. It will certainly come as the form of friendship losses, losing jobs and financial security, denied access to services and benefits, and the use of lawsuits against any who oppose the wicked agendas which will come upon the world, hating anything springing from godly rightness.

In verse 14, Jesus said the gospel will be preached to the world for a witness to all nations and then the end would come. Remember, every jot and tittle in God's Word is important and must come to pass. We can easily overlook details and cues when our focus is on another aspect of the passage. Often our focus goes to certain words and phrases in a verse and passage and we overlook other important terms. Let's look particularly verses 29–31 (NIV).

> Immediately after the distress of those days 'the sun will be darkened, and the moon will not give its light; the stars will fall from the sky, and the heavenly bodies will be shaken.' "Then will appear the sign of the Son of Man in heaven. And then all the peoples of the earth will mourn when they see the Son of Man coming on the clouds of heaven, with power and great glory. And he will send his angels with a loud trumpet call, and they will gather his elect from the four winds, from one end of the heavens to the other.

Verses 29–31 sequentially list events showing His return was imminent. How did He do this? He used terms of sequence. Terms of sequence point out timing, next in order of time, actions or events, and can explain the past, present, or foretell future events. It can also mean *at that time.* Sequential term examples are: before, aforementioned, previous, therefore, after, afterwards, next and then, just to name a few. In my aforementioned example, I used the term *then* to signify when I would return. Jesus used the same term when He answered His disciples' question regarding His return and the last days, and so Jesus' own statements are the most compelling, as they should be premiere regarding anything. The term *then* can also mean 'at that same time' depending on its use. Now if the term *then* as found in verses 9, 16, 21 and 23 meant 'at that time', it would suggest all the events listed from verse 5 through verse 28 would occur during the days of tribulation. Jesus stated in verse 21, "For then shall be great tribulation," which can be read, "For *at that time* shall be great tribulation." Then it would mean for all things listed from verse 5 through verse 28 should occur during the days of tribulation, or they will additionally happen during the great tribulation. To say they will occur as well during the great tribulation, I say, yes, they will. Now if we believe verses 21–28 will occur during the great tribulation due to verse 21 saying, "For then shall be great tribulation . . ." we would have to concede the tribulation goes at least from verse 15 through to 31. Why from verse 15? Because the 'abomination that makes desolation' referenced in Daniel 9 and 12, is a key marker of the tribulation period. This element alone is not an indicator to the rapture. Either way, it is key.

Jesus particularly said the days of great tribulation will be such not seen since the beginning of the world to this time, nor ever will be. Therefore, we must acknowledge Jesus marked the great tribulation in this chapter. He didn't specify hour or day, but timing in order and reference to other events. Obviously, we can see Jesus predicted His return during the tribulation by the terms of sequence He used. Let's go further because He said more.

CHAPTER FIVE

CELESTIAL SIGNS

S ome of the most notable visual clues during the tribulation period will be celestial signs. These don't mark the rapture's proximity, but what we know according to Jesus, is that they occur before He returns. Joel prophesied this in 3:14–15 (ESV), "Multitudes, multitudes in the valley of decision! For the day of the LORD is near in the valley of decision. The sun and moon will be darkened, and the stars withdraw their shining."

It is unknown how long during the tribulation period these astronomic signs will persist, but their beginnings will occur before the rapture. How do we know this? Jesus foretold the future and He was specific. Matthew recorded Jesus Christ saying in 24:29, the sun will darken, and the moon will not give its light, stars shall fall from heaven, and the powers of the heavens will shake immediately after the great adversity of those days. Verse 29 alone does not announce the rapture, but its sequential placement to verses 30 and 31 situates it. You will see in a moment. Notice He said " . . . after the tribulation of those days . . ."

After denotes sequence. After the tribulation of what days? After the tribulation of the days Jesus mentioned previous to verse 29, these cosmic calamities will ensue. In Revelation 6:12–14, the vision John saw matched the prophecy Jesus spoke, wherein the sun turns black and moon as blood, stars fall, and heavens depart as a scroll. To people of that day, these foretold sightings could have been unimaginable and thought to be only symbolic. We know these are literal and can happen by the solar eclipses, blood moons, falling stars, and the scientific space exploration seen in our lifetimes.

Furthermore, in Revelation, we will also see in 7:1 that no wind will blow; in 8:7–12, there will be hail and fire with blood; the seas become blood; Wormwood, an enormous asteroid, will fall and one-third of the sun, moon and stars will darken.

I was a science major when I attended college in my twenties. Any science major knows you spend a lot of time in the science building and library. One afternoon I was reading a science periodical, *Science Digest*. I came across a short column article regarding a newly discovered, large asteroid buzzing around out in space. The scientists interviewed theorized it might come precariously close to the Earth's atmosphere some time in the future. Incidentally, the scientists who made the discovery named it Wormwood. That can't be a coincidence. I regret not purchasing the magazine to keep for future sermons and book reference. This shows science corroborates Scripture, as it often does.

These incidences definitely are cataclysmic. We might doubt smaller prophecies that come to fruition in another place to other people, explaining them away as coincidence, rare fluke or freak accident. These will be astronomic mega signs. And for them all to occur together and be foretold with accuracy, what are the statistical chances?

What God is doing in the tribulation is 'turning up the volume' above the world's enchantment in one last-ditch effort so people will acknowledge Him and repent to be saved.

Remember, one big lesson is the Lord Jesus is in control of all these marvels. He calls all the shots throughout the Revelation narrative. Nothing will happen outside His permission. Everything is under supreme power and will kneel to His majesty.

Indeed, these celestial signs are epic markers He forecasted would happen before His return and the Church's rapture.

Ah, Sovereign Lord, you have made heaven and earth by your great power and outstretched arm. Nothing is too hard for you. (Jer. 32:17)

CHAPTER SIX

THE ELECTS SAKE

If those days had not been cut short, no one would survive, but for the sake of the elect those days will be shortened. At that time if anyone says to you, 'Look, here is the Messiah!' or, 'There he is!' do not believe it. For false messiahs and false prophets will appear and perform great signs and wonders to deceive, if possible, even the elect. See, I have told you ahead of time. (Matt. 24:22, 24 [NIV])

We should admit, Jesus stated out of His own mouth, those details in verses 5 through 21 of Matthew's Gospel will occur during the tribulation as well. Now, we move on to these two verses. Catching my attention are His references to *those days* and to *the elect*.

Consequently, who are the elect? εκλεκτός (eklektos) is the Greek word for *elect*. It means chosen, elect; and by implication—favorite. Ekklesia is the Greek collective term for the Church, the called-out ones; saints. We can see the two terms are related.

We should recognize *those days* of adversity will be shortened for the elect's sake, in verses 22 and 24. Now, if the elect are raptured before the days of tribulation, why did Jesus say the days would be shortened for their sake if they weren't on earth? Why say false Christs might delude the very elect, if it were possible? If the elect are absent, what need is there for the days shortening? And why specifically mention the possibility that phony Christs might deceive the elect? Obviously, the elect will still be on earth during this time of tribulation. With close reading comprehension, verses 22 through 24 tie to verse 21 because verse 22 said, "And except [or unless] those days be shortened . . ." Part of His phrase, "And except *those* days" links back to the days mentioned in verse 21.

This one Greek word found in *Strong's Concordance* for *elect* is also used in Mark 13:22, 27; Luke 18:7; Romans 8:33; Colossians 3:12; Titus 1:1; First Peter 1:2, 2:6; Second John 1, 13; Second Timothy 2:10.[1] In each instance, it means the same. In each occasion and context, there is no allusion about end-times or the Revelation 144 thousand evangelistic Jews. 'Elect' referred to Christian brethren in the general sense in these passages. According to the aforementioned verses referencing *elect*, the word pertained to Christians of that day by those writers. Therefore, Jesus' reference to 'elect' cannot refer *only* to the 144,000 Jews found in Revelation, as some speculate. For any who believe God already raptured the saints by this time and those remaining are the 144 thousand Jews, I ask, *are you sure?* If the rapture supposedly occurs before this point, when did it happen and when do these 144 thousand get raptured then in Revelation? Is there any description or evidence to such? No other rapture is mentioned. Scriptures signify the rapture is a single episode. A notion of two separate raptures, one at Revelation 4:1–2 and one later for those saved during the Tribulation, just doesn't jive in God's Word. People will *conceive* other supposed details when their human logic and understanding disagree with the Bible.

Consider Jesus' words. The gospel writers record He indicated *a* gathering up: single, not plural. In First Thessalonians 4:17–18, Paul's rapture description is also singular. Sometimes what we have been taught conflicts with biblical truth. I've been there many times. I decided my belief had to align with the evidence, whether I liked what it said and no matter what anyone previously taught me. Let's continue with the days being shortened for the elect's sake.

Can days actually shorten? Is this possible? They can. After the great tsunami slammed into Japan on March 11, 2011, scientists determined the massive undersea earthquake causing it was so powerful it caused the earth to speed up its rotation, unnoticeably to us, shortening the day. Here's scientific proof a day (s) can shorten. Will the days be shortened the same way? How is He going to shorten the days for the elect's sake? I don't know. That's up to Him. He definitely can do it and is going to do it.

Thank You, Lord, for Your kind grace by shortening the days.

THE THREAT OF DECEPTION

Continuing, believers should be aware of the added potential fraud. Jesus warned His disciples of malignant messiahs arising so they and we wouldn't be deceived. Signs and wonders by any declaring 'this is the Christ' or a saviour, He said, *don't believe them.*

Today, believers can perform valid miracles by the power of the Holy Spirit. I have seen many performed by the Lord's permission and power over the last few years—dozens and dozens of miraculous healings, and we will see more wonders increase in the coming years. However, these beguiling prophets and malevolent messiahs will declare themselves to be Christ or others will declare them to be so. Take note, any who are on earth declaring to be Christ and performing signs and wonders, are not. We know His coming will be lightning fast (Matt. 24:27), appearing in the clouds to take up His people, not performing signs and wonders on the earth claiming to be a Christ. There's the simple way to tell the difference between a corrupt Christ and the real Christ; they will be on earth—He will come in the clouds. We can't mistake that! Like buzzards and eagles gather around carcasses, so will people gather around these. So don't be fooled by masses of people surrounding persons claiming to be a messiah who have powers, and abilities, and speak charismatically. They aren't valid just because people assemble around them.

Moving on, Matthew 24:29 says:

Immediately *after* the tribulation of *those days* 'the sun will be darkened, and the moon will not give its light; the stars will fall from the sky, and the heavenly bodies will be shaken.' (Emphasis added).

Jesus said *immediately after*. *Immediately after* indicates something follows in sequence rapidly. Immediately after what? The tribulation of those days. *Those* designates specific days. Which days? The days previously referred to which include the elect being present on the earth. So when we look at the events mentioned earlier in the passage by Jesus, He said *after* them would follow what He described next—the darkened sun, decreased luminosity of the moon; stars will fall from the sky, and the celestial bodies will shudder.

Now look at what Jesus said in Matthew 24:30–31,

> *Then* will appear the sign of the Son of Man in heaven. And then all the peoples of the earth will mourn when they see the Son of Man coming on the clouds of heaven, with power and great glory. And he will send his angels with a loud trumpet call, and they will gather his elect from the four winds, from one end of the heavens to the other. (Emphasis added)

What are the elements of these two verses? Jesus will appear in the clouds, people will mourn, there will be a loud trumpet sound, and angels will gather the elect up. That's how Matthew heard it. Let's read how Mark and Luke heard it.

Mark documented Jesus saying 13:24–27,

> But in those days, following that tribulation, 'the sun will be darkened, and the moon will not give its light; the stars will fall from the sky, and the heavenly bodies will be shaken.' "At that time people will see the Son of Man coming in clouds with great power and glory. *And then* will send his angels and gather his elect from the four winds, from the ends of the earth to the ends of the heavens. (Emphasis mine)

Now for Luke's dictation:

> There will be signs in the sun, moon and stars. On the
> earth, nations will be in anguish and perplexity at the
> roaring and tossing of the sea. People will faint from
> terror, apprehensive of what is coming on the world, for
> the heavenly bodies will be shaken. At that time they will
> see the Son of Man coming in a cloud with power and
> great glory. When these things begin to take place, stand
> up and lift up your heads, because your redemption is
> drawing near. (Luke 21:25, 27–28 [NIV])

Each writer's instance reads with the same graphic
details of His return and the rapture. Each gospel writer
chronicled Jesus stating identical actual markers of the
tribulation period that will occur before He returns to
gather up His elect. Because all three testimonies agree,
they must be accurate. This report of Jesus' words, therefore, is incontestable.

Later, we will search for where these elements occur in
Revelation. Consider what Peter said in Acts 2:17–20
(NIV),

> In the last days, God says, I will pour out my Spirit on all
> people. Your sons and daughters will prophesy, your
> young men will see visions, your old men will dream
> dreams. Even on my servants, both men and women, I
> will pour out my Spirit in those days, and they will
> prophesy. I will show wonders in the heavens above and
> signs on the earth below, blood and fire and billows of
> smoke. The sun will be turned to darkness and the moon
> to blood before the coming of the great and glorious day

of the Lord. And everyone who calls on the name of the Lord will be saved.

Luke, the writer of Acts, recorded Peter quoting this prophetic word from the prophet Joel's book 2:28 through 30. It begins 'In the last days . . . ' with the signs of fire, blood, smoke, the sun darkened, the moon turning the color of blood.

To summarize; these heavenly signs will ensue, the elect will be present on the earth, and the days will be abbreviated. All the descriptors Jesus foretold will occur before He returns.

CHAPTER SEVEN

APOSTLE PAUL'S CLUES

W hat Jesus prophesied about His return in the first three Gospels, Apostle Paul also mirrored in his letters. Let's start in First Thessalonians 4:13–18 (NIV). Here, Paul wrote,

> Brothers and sisters, we do not want you to be unin-formed about those who sleep in death, so that you do not grieve like the rest of mankind, who have no hope. For we believe that Jesus died and rose again, and so we believe that God will bring with Jesus those who have fallen asleep in him . . . we tell you that we who are still alive, who are left until the coming of the Lord, will certainly not precede those who have fallen asleep. For the Lord himself will come down from heaven, with a loud command, with the voice of the archangel and with the trumpet call of God, and the dead in Christ will rise first. After that, we who are still alive and are left will be caught up together with them in the clouds to meet the

Lord in the air. And so we will be with the Lord forever.
Therefore encourage one another with these words.

Paul listed the components of the rapture: the Son of Man's appearance and descent in the clouds, an archangel loudly commands, and a trumpet sounds. Then all believers are taken up. Those dead 'in Christ' will be raised first, and then those who are still alive at His appearing will follow instantly, faster than 5G. So far, Paul's rapture depiction matches exactly with what Jesus said in the Gospels; He descends and is seen in the clouds and air, an angel shouts, a trumpet sounds, and believers are gathered to meet Him in the clouds and air. The difference Paul mentions is a detail of order in who is taken up first in this one and same event. He didn't distinguish as a separate event, those dead in Christ rising first from those alive who immediately will follow, but spoke of it as the one and same ordered collection. Obviously, Jesus and Paul's prophetic testimonies agree and it is these predictive elements that we look for in Revelation.

CHAPTER EIGHT

REVELATION FOUR

W hat about Revelation 4:1–2? Isn't that the rapture? It's what I've always heard. It's before the tribulation begins. Some say so. Well, let's look at it.

Apostle John is the author of the last book of the Bible, Revelation. Like a secretary, he took dictation directly from Jesus, assembling the first three chapters. You can't get any truer first-hand information than that, right? Following these, he wrote everything shown and expressed to him in the subsequent visions in heaven, except where he was advised in Revelation 10:4, *don't write this down.*

Remember, the clues that precede the rapture recorded from Jesus and read from Paul's letter are these: the Son of Man will descend, appear in the clouds and in the air, an archangel will shout a command, the last trumpet blares, and saints are snatched up. These are the elements we search for in Revelation. So we must ask ourselves, where do these described events take place in the book of Revelation?

I know preachers, who held a certain view, teach Revelation 4:1–2 is where the rapture takes place. The reason I think they did so is that they were taught so and, people want to believe in an adversity-free life. One author said 'one may appropriately identify John's call up to heaven as a rapture event'.[1] But I disagree that one may appropriately identify this as a rapture event. Why? How can one appropriately identify this as a rapture event? Just saying it does not make it correct. No passage about the rapture ever mentions John or anything about him receiving this Revelation 4:1–2 vision. Therefore, one cannot duly identify John's call up to heaven as the rapture incident. You will see why there is biblical disagreement.

In particular, some people consider it to be so because the apostle John heard a voice that sounded like a trumpet saying, "Come up here." They assume it meant a call to meet Jesus in the air; hence, it must be the rapture. That's the assumption persons have taken about the verses. I don't doubt their good intentions, nor do I think any intend to mislead; however, I just think this premise has been accepted without inspection.

In Acts 17:11, the Bereans were a people Paul encountered who didn't just accept anything they were told but studied to see 'whether those things were so' and for this, Paul called them noble. No matter who teaches what from the Bible, including me, we need to be 'noble Bereans' and neutrally check it out ourselves. Let's delve into this passage.

BREAKING DOWN REVELATION 4:1–2

We're going to walk through this 4:1–2 passage with several points made. In Revelation 4:1, John wrote 'After this . . . '

After what? After receiving this dictation from Jesus about the seven churches of Asia, beginning with Revelation 2:1 through to the end of Revelation 3. (Be careful about letting chapter breaks interrupt the flow of what is written). I continue with the text Revelation 4:1–2 (NIV).

> After this I looked, and there before me was a door standing open in heaven. And the voice I had first heard speaking to me like a trumpet said, "Come up here, and I will show you what must take place after this."At once I was in the Spirit, and there before me was a throne in heaven with someone sitting on it.

After dictating chapters 1–3, John noted in chapter 4 that he looked. Often throughout Scripture and today, people who see visions and dreams do so with the eyes of their heart or 'spiritual eyes'. How John did, we aren't sure. No matter really, because John saw what he saw, and that matters most for this study.

In this moment, he is on earth seeing a vision. And what was the vision? It was of a portal opened in heaven. He wasn't ushered yet into heaven, but he saw the opening in heaven for him to come through.

Next, he heard a voice. He didn't hear a trumpet but a voice 'as it were of a trumpet'; or by the NIV, the voice he first heard speaking was *like* a trumpet. Notably, it was a voice John heard. He heard a voice earlier speak to him like a trumpet (Rev. 1:10), yet no one ever claims it as the rapture. We can't assume because he heard a voice like a trumpet in Revelation 4:1 that it must be the rapture event. The voice was resonant. In all likelihood, its sound carried like a trumpet's would. Nevertheless, it was a voice John heard, not a trumpet. Incidentally, this simile is the only figurative speech in the passage, and therefore, leaves very little room for symbolic interpretation.

It isn't said whose voice it was. It could very well have been Jesus' voice, but this doesn't affect the content of what was said and the details of John's experience. Moreover, the voice said, "Come up here". Now, those are pleasing words to hear for anyone, especially when *here* is heaven. This is where some bible scholars and writers end the sentence. There's no grammatical period ending the statement here but a comma because the charge to John isn't complete. The complete command from the voice is, "Come up here, and I will show you what must take place after this" (NIV). The King James Version reads, "Come up hither, and I will shew thee things which must be hereafter." Pretty identical verses, wouldn't you say? The voice didn't say 'come up here' *only*, but additionally "*and* I will show what must take place after this."

Now let's recap. John saw a vision of a portal open in heaven and heard a voice say, "Come up here, and I will show you what must take place after this."

First, this can't be the rapture because Jesus and Paul both said we would meet Jesus in the air and clouds, not heaven. There are neither clouds mentioned here nor any meeting in the air. We'll eventually get to heaven, but our initial meeting with Jesus is in the clouds and in the air, not heaven. This voice is commanding John to come up to heaven.

Second point: incomplete reading comprehension. The voice didn't say only "Come up here," period. That would be poor grammar to cut off and ignore the rest of the statement " . . . and I will show you what must take place after this."

Correctly and literally, the invitation is for John only to *come up here and let me tell you what happens next.* John is the only one addressed and acknowledged. Otherwise, if this would be the rapture, the directive would have to be for us and all other believers as well as John, that we should come up and we be told what will happen next, too. Remarkably, this is not the only place in Revelation where the phrase *come up here* was uttered. I found it repeated in Revelation 11:12. We should examine that instance, right? Let's investigate in the vision to whom it was conveyed and where *here* is.

In Revelation 11:12, the two prophets, who in chapter 11 were given power to stop rain and perform miracles, were commanded to 'Come up here'. *Here* in the command to them was heaven, the same as it was for John. Furthermore, this order to *come up* does not coincide with any rapture elements. There is no angel shout, no Jesus descending in the clouds and no collection of saints seen at this moment. Since none of them occur, we can safely rule out this verbal command to *come up here* is not a marker for the rapture. Besides, no biblical character or biblical writer ever said these words would be spoken pertaining to the event. This doesn't mean they wouldn't be, but we can't assume the words *come up here* will be said at our collection, since no Scripture notes such beforehand.

Third point: two raptures for John? If this verse were the literal rapture, then it makes little sense that we, and John, would be called up but he be the only one who then gets the vision again for him to record anew, thus replaying future history. It would be like an episode out of the movie

Back To The Future II where the character Marty McFly goes back and forth to the future, then back to the past or present and reappears again in the future.[2] John being called and taken up in the spirit into heaven actually happened, past tense without us, therefore, it can't be a future event for him again and include us.

Fourth reason: John called up in spirit. In verse 2, John recorded he was immediately in the spirit, not bodily flesh, when he appeared in heaven and saw visions unfold. If this were the rapture event, John should have been taken up physically in body, but he wasn't. Jesus said believers would be taken up bodily, and as Paul affirmed, as our bodies will change from corruptible to incorruptible in the rapture, which does not happen to John.

Fifth reason: incongruent reality. If this were the real rapture, then John was the only one raptured because we are still here now on earth, or it would mean Apostle John has not died yet but is alive somewhere here on earth awaiting to be taken up with us together. History has already recorded John's death circa 98 AD. If Revelation 4:1–2 was the real rapture at John's experience back then, he wouldn't be on earth past chapter 4 to leave behind the rest of the book of Revelation in print. If he and believers were raptured then, that would place our existence now at least one thousand years past the millennial reign, which we obviously are not.

Sixth reason: no trumpet series occurs by Revelation 4:2. John mentioned no actual trumpet or series of trumpets being blown near or up to this point in Revelation. Paul and Jesus asserted a trumpet blast is an element occurring before or at the rapture. John heard a voice, which sounded *like* a trumpet. The only series of trumpets blown in Revelation occurs during the tribulation period. We'll come back to that later.

Lastly: John's experience doesn't match Jesus and Paul's description. These verses mention nothing of Jesus descending in the clouds and the air, or of other believers being taken up, or of an angel shouting at Revelation 4:1–2. Nothing in these verses shows the rapture occurring. It makes no sense, nor does it correlate to any of the literal, descriptive details of the rapture event Jesus and Paul told. A literal interpretation depicts no rapture elements Jesus and Paul described. A figurative interpretation must do some real scripture-stretching to even make it fit.

This chapter and verse cannot be where it occurs. The pre-trib authors's books I've read said they came to their conclusions based on literal interpretation[3]. Yet, when it came to this passage, they didn't interpret it literally. John's spirit call to heaven can't be construed as the rapture prefacing the Tribulation Period. It's with inaccurate grammar and reading comprehension to construe these verses as the rapture, or it's a conscious intentional denial or simple rejection of believing the rapture happens later in Revelation.

Finally, there is no reason in this passage, or in any other verse, to suggest or imagine the claim by some that the apostle John represents the Church. The misinterpretation of these verses in Revelation as the rapture event, literally or figuratively, is inaccurate and a biased, non-literal stretch.

CHAPTER NINE

THE LAST TRUMPET

One of the most notable markers to the rapture is the last trumpet sound. In the Old Testament, trumpets were common and an integral part of local and national life in Israel. Watchmen blew alarms when towns and cities were under attack. They were used to signal various commands on the battlefield. Trumpets, as well as other instruments, were integral to temple worship for ceremonies, calling for assemblies, and national festivals (Num. 10:2–3).[1] Certain trumpet blasts communicated certain messages. In all these uses, worship services and festivals, the primary use of the trumpet was for communicating over distance because its sound carried far and loudly. In First Corinthians 15:51–54 (NIV) Paul wrote,

> Listen, I tell you a mystery: We will not all sleep, but we will all be changed—in a flash, in the twinkling of an eye, at the last trumpet. For the trumpet will sound, the dead will be raised imperishable, and we will be changed. For the perishable must clothe itself with the imperishable,

and the mortal with immortality. When the perishable has been clothed with the imperishable, and the mortal with immortality, then the saying that is written will come true: "Death has been swallowed up in victory."

The first clue Paul gave is here. He said the raising and changing of believers in the rapture is a mystery. How wonderful! In a flash, in the blink of an eye our corruptible bodies will change to incorruptible ones. Amen! So, Paul said in this verse, God will change all believers physically. The apostle John agreed, "Dear friends, now we are children of God, and what we will be has not yet been made known. But we know that when Christ appears, we shall be like him, for we shall see him as he is" (1 John 3:2).

In Exodus 33:18 through 23, Moses asked God to let him see His glory. God replied by saying He would make all His goodness pass before Moses. Obviously then, the glory of God is directly connected to and is a result of His goodness. His goodness is so good it's glorious. And because God was going to let His *entire* goodness pass before Moses (that's got to be some super goodness), Moses needed protection. When God told Him "no man can see my face and live", it wasn't a threat. God was saying (I paraphrase), *Because all of My goodness is so incredibly powerful, Moses, in your present humanness your body can't take it. I need to protect you by covering you with My hand.* From then on, in public, Moses had to cover his face because it shone so brightly. A reason we will be given a new body is because these natural bodies can't take the power of all God's goodness.

When will we be like Him with a new resurrected, incorruptible body? When He appears at the rapture. In another letter chapter, Paul compared what will happen with those believers who have been dead to those who are alive when Christ returns and the trumpet sounds. He makes no sign in the passage when the rapture will occur but unveils the bodily change while raptured. When will the rapture occur? Paul said at the timing of the last trumpet sound.

The second clue is the last trumpet sound. When the trumpet sounds, the dead will be raised imperishable, and those alive will be changed (1 Cor.15:51–52). For there to be a last trumpet, there must be other trumpets blown before that final one.

There are two significant trumpet soundings in the Bible. One occurs during the Old Testament festival, Feast of Trumpets, coinciding in Rosh Hashanah in September each year. There are four kinds of trumpet blasts during this festival; tekiah, shevarim, truah and tekiah gedolah. These festival blasts are many: one hundred in total.[2] Tekiah, shevarim and truah blast thirty-three times each with tekiah gedolah as the last, longest, and the one-hundreth blast. Does this mean in the year the rapture occurs, it will happen during this festival week? It's very possible it will coincide with it, and I think it will. I'm declined to think this last, one-hundreth burst is the significant one indicated by Paul. However, I think the tekiah gedolah blast on earth, in whatever year it will be, will coincide with that significant angel-blown trumpet discussed next.

THE LAST TRUMPET

The second significant trumpet series blown in the Bible occurs in Revelation. John specified seven trumpets blown by angels loudly, signifying globally universal events occurring rather than those only heard locally in Israel. This isn't to confuse, again, a voice sounding like a trumpet.

Where do the seven trumpets sound in Revelation? Beginning in Revelation 8:7, we find the first trumpet; in 8:8, the second trumpet; in 8:10, the third trumpet blast; at 8:12, the fourth trumpet; in 9:1, the fifth trumpet sound; at 9:13, the sixth trumpet's peal and then the seventh and last trumpet blast. So, the clue we look for is when the last trumpet sounds. Where in Revelations does it occur? Answer: Revelation 11:15.

> The seventh angel sounded his trumpet, and there were loud voices in heaven, which said: "The kingdom of the world has become the kingdom of our Lord and of his Messiah, and he will reign for ever and ever."

At this trumpet sound, angels in heaven spoke out loudly. They didn't do this with the previous six blasts. For this reason, its significance is obvious, as it will coordinate with the seventh angel blowing it. So, is this where the rapture occurs? Paul said, 'at the last trumpet sound'.

The meaning of the term *at* varies. By example, saying *I'll meet you at the County Fair* still doesn't communicate precisely when I will. Will I see you at its outset, somewhere in the middle or near its finish? My statement isn't clear enough, right? As long as I meet you there, I have fulfilled what I said. Let me give you another illustration. If I say I'll see you at graduation, what do I exactly mean? Graduation ceremonies commence on a certain day, time, and place. Convocations can last several hours. If we met anytime from its beginning or near the end, we could attest we met at graduation. This is an example of prophetic delay where the fulfillment of the prophecy is not simultaneous with the sign. It is not necessarily conveyed that at the exact moment the trumpet sound is heard hanging in the air (the sign) the rapture will occur (the fulfillment associated with the sign). Let's continue.

> But in the days when the seventh angel is about to sound his trumpet, the mystery of God will be accomplished, just as he announced to his servants the prophets. (Rev. 10:7 [NIV])

In the above verse, John wrote "in the days of the voice of the seventh angel, when he shall begin his sound . . . " Notice it says in the *days*, plural. It may be this angel's cry and trumpet sounding may last awhile, on a day or over days. Note that John said when the angel *is about* to sound his trumpet. This marks this trumpet as significant because it is synchronous with God's mysterious plan's attainment. This is extremely consequential. Whether it coordinates with the Feast of Trumpets, we'll see. It could, and I think it will. But undoubtedly, this is the 'last trumpet' foretold because of the notable drama coordinated with His plan's fulfillment and the kingdom of the world becoming His kingdom. Because there has been great anticipation through the ages for its culmination, we cannot overstate its importance. This is what God has waited for!

What is this hidden, inexplicable plan? To undo what came through the first Adam, redeem a people to be with Him forever, and unite Jew and Gentile in Him once and for all under His banner and in Him (Eph.1:9, 3:3–9).

Before the cross, the Spirit of God would come upon people for a time, do His work with them, then leave. That was the *visitation of God experience.* But post the cross of Jesus, God no longer came and went but inhabited the person and never left. Colossians 1:26–27 (NIV) says,

> " . . . the mystery that has been kept hidden for ages and generations, but is now disclosed to the Lord's people. To them God has chosen to make known among the Gentiles the glorious riches of this mystery, which is Christ in you, the hope of glory."

So then, the mystery of God is that God no longer visits you but inhabits you and never leaves. The Cross institutes the *habitation of God experience.* That's the experiential culture we live in now. This is the mystery that was hidden.

So what is *the fullness* of the mystery of God? The fullness, or the finishing, of the mystery is when all who will receive Christ's indwelling Spirit, do. It is when all who will be saved, are saved, and the mystery of God has reached capacity. This is what the trumpet signals, that it is time to gather all His people, all at once. This is also why the rapture cannot happen at Revelation 4:1–2. Only when the mystery is accomplished will the gathering take place. This is why the mystery of God and the rapture are connected.

And so, God will culminate the mystery's fulfillment with the rapture. This clarion signals the long-awaited crescendo and why it is so momentous in the Bible and creation's history.

TIME ELAPSE AFTER THE LAST TRUMPET

As we read verses before and after chapter 11:15, we should ask, do we see a description of the rapture happening? The answer is, no, we don't—not in this verse and moment. It is uncertain exactly how long it sounds, but do we see a rapture description coinciding at, with, or around the last trumpet blast? If we do, it still scripturally agrees with *at the last trumpet*. Again, we're looking for all four markers: the last trumpet sound in close scriptural proximity to Jesus' descent, an archangel shout, and the gathering up, to fit Jesus and Paul's descriptions.

Following this last trumpet sound through chapter 11's end is a string of pronouncements in heaven, outside relation to earthly time. During those proclamations, we don't know how much time elapses on earth, if any. In some of the heavenly visions, it is uncertain exactly how much time passes on earth, unless otherwise indicated.

Chapter 12 is another vision seen by John. He called it a great wonder that moved him with awe. It contains big-picture, allegorically and literally layered illustrations. The large imagery depicts hidden, behind-the-scene spiritual events during creation's approximately six-thousand year history in one abbreviated, broad-scope movie. This feature presentation starts with the flashback of Lucifer's fall from heaven and his many attempts to harm the female personifications of Eve/Israel/Zion and her offspring (Jesus and the Church) at points in the past, the present and future, wrapping up in the future-present as chapter 12 ends and 13 begins.

We can't be sure how much time spans while the vision is shown to John in heaven or on the earth in the future-present as the chapter narrative progresses from the chapter's introduction through its end, moving into chapter 13. Having said this, it seems the earthly interval from the last trumpet in chapter 11 to chapter 13's beginning is very short, if any time elapses at all. (Perhaps this is the time the days are shortened for the elect's sake.)

(Note: The second woe ends just before this last trumpet in Revelations 11:15; and, with the third woe coming, this trumpet is positioned undoubtedly during the Tribulation.) (You read how I couple Jesus and Paul's rapture descriptions. I don't make Paul's words equal to Jesus's but mention them alongside His simply because his narrative aligns with Jesus's.)

In conclusion, we must be very close to where the rapture ensues in Revelation because we read here the seventh, last and significant trumpet sounds in Revelation 11:15, one of the remaining four markers. Can you feel the tension mount?

CHAPTER TEN

MORE CLUES FROM PAUL

P aul provided more information for believers and I'm glad he did. Where the next clue takes us to is found in Second Thessalonians 2:1–4 (NIV), picking up in verse 1, "Concerning the coming of our Lord Jesus Christ and our being gathered to him, we ask you, brothers and sisters, . . ."

What do we see here? Paul stated the subject he wanted to discuss: Jesus' wonderful return and our gathering to Him.

Gathering is an agricultural reference for harvesting. This word 'gathering' translated *episunagōgē* in the Greek, means 'a complete collection or collecting in the same place'.[1] So what is this, our being gathered? It is the harvest of us, His believers—our rapture, and pointedly, a complete collection of believers, alive and dead, which also takes place from the same place, earth. Now, verse 2.

...not to become easily unsettled or alarmed by the teaching allegedly from us—whether by a prophecy or by word of mouth or by letter— asserting that the day of the

Lord has already come. 'Don't let anyone deceive you in any way.' (2 Thess. 2:2–3a NIV),

and;

. . . for you know very well that the day of the Lord will come like a thief in the night...But you, brothers and sisters, are not in darkness so that this day should surprise you like a thief. (1 Thessalonians 5:2, 4 NIV)

Paul encouraged the Thessalonians to not anxiously look about nor precariously waver by deceptive teachings. A rumor circulated the rapture had already happened due to sufferings, intolerances, and persecutions. Thinking the rapture occurred could easily delude them. And in First Thessalonians 5:2, 4, he said we shouldn't be surprised by it. Those in darkness will be surprised when it happens because they will be unprepared (unsaved).

People will deceive, saying Jesus came and went. It wouldn't be surprising if this same lie were retold. If it is, remember, Christian, you haven't been left and you haven't missed it. I paraphrase Paul's words, *Do not worry. It hasn't happened yet and you won't be forsaken. Let me give you a couple of markers so you will know when it is nearer.* I resume to Second Thessalonians 2:3 (NIV), 'Don't let anyone deceive you in any way, for *that day* will not come until the rebellion occurs and the man of lawlessness is revealed . . .' (Emphasis added).

Now the clues from Second Thessalonians 2:3 are: that day, until, the rebellion, and the man of lawlessness is revealed.

What day? The day of Jesus's return and our being gathered together to him. Everything I've read on all sides of the debate agree 'our being gathered to Him' references the rapture. Notice Paul coupled both Christ's coming and our gathering to 'that day', a specific single day or a singular time.

Day can but doesn't necessarily mean a twenty-four-hour period. In the Greek language, *day* can also represent a period of time, or an age in which something comes to pass. In this case, it also means one of the latter, as we will see.

First, let's consider the two clues. Paul said the rebellion occurs before 'that day' comes. The King James Version uses 'falling away' instead of 'rebellion'. What is the rebellion, or falling away? Some say this means *Christians will fall away from the faith and lose their salvation, and so it must be because you can't lose salvation unless you're a believer.* Not so. That would be a double whammy if it were true. Let's let the Bible say what it says and not read into it. No express wording says Christians or only Christians will fall away from the faith. It says *some* shall depart from the faith (1 Tim. 4:1). Will any be Christians? Possibly.

There are two different meanings for 'falling away' in the New Testament. One means to be offended. Like the disciples who fell away at Jesus' trial, were offended because of Him because they were associated with the ridiculed and shamed Jesus (Mark 14:27 [ESV]). Because many wanted Him dead, the disciples thought they might suffer His same fate. Peter denied Jesus. This word *deny* means to abstain or utterly disown. In this sense, anyone could be offended for associating with Jesus. In their offence and Peter's denial, Jesus did not forsake them but *kept them.* I want to note that 'falling away' does not mean losing salvation. If it did, it would be a violation of God's 'holding power' to save.

The second definition is apostasy, or rebellion. Again, no word here refers *only* to believers, so let's not read into it. It is a generic, broad dissent. This rebellion is a turning away, a defection from whatever is righteous, godly, or of God. It will be a worldwide societal abandonment of God and belief in Him. For some, it will be their choice to reject things related to God because of the influence and force of the antichrist/anti-Christian agenda. For others, it will be a subtle misleading. Both ways are deceptive.

There will be some who were following the faith but withdrew themselves, like a military deserter would do. Luke 8:13 says the seed that fell on the rocky soil withered because it had no root. Jesus' explanation was these were those who received the word but fell away in the time of testing (tribulation).

There will be ones who are faithful believers, allegiant to the Lord. In Matthew 25:1–13 Jesus told the parable of the Ten Virgins. It's about readiness for the Bridegroom's return, and about truly knowing Him and He, them. Five virgins, the bridegroom knew; five, he didn't know. It will be seen who is and isn't true, thus, the saying will play out 'they went out from us because they were never of us'.

There will be many who ignorantly follow fake Christs, and with so many distorted images of Jesus in the world today, it's no wonder. Religion can do that—distort the true nature and character of God by any deviation from the Plumb Line, the One True Person of Jesus Christ. Even people who participate in occult religions will tell you they believe in Jesus. In my ministry work, I've learned to ask them, *which Jesus do you believe in?* And *what do you mean when you say you believe in Him?*

Jesus said in Matthew 7:22–23, on that day many will plead with Him, professing to have done wonderful works in His name but He will say He never knew them. I've heard one pastor use this verse to prove people can lose salvation. That's not the case. Jesus said He *never* knew them. He didn't say He knew them then forgot them. This means they were never saved to begin with. People can believe God exists but not really know Him personally or be known by Him. In James' letter, he said even demons believe in God and tremble, and we know they won't be saved. Paul said this 'turning away' has to happen before Christ comes and we are gathered. It doesn't mean everyone will abandon believing in God but that many will.

The knowledge 'that God exists' among people has been declining. There are many who still believe in God's existence throughout much of the world but it's decreasing. Christians and Christian living will be seen as the aberrant virus program in the *Matrix* that needs to be defragged and reprogrammed.[2] Really. In the spring of 2020 when the pandemic started and BLM was on the rampage, some American left-wing politicians made statements before TV news reporters to the effect that some people need to be reprogrammed. What? Reprogrammed?! This is all part of 'the turning away' and the powers behind the anti-Christ system that do not want any to buck the system. Apostle Paul gave a warning way back then in this verse so we wouldn't be alarmed today as it continues.

Next, Paul said before Christ comes and gathers us, the man of lawlessness, or son of perdition, must be revealed. Second Thessalonians 2:3 (NIV) says ' . . . for *that day* will not come *until* the rebellion occurs *and* the man of lawlessness is revealed,' (Emphasis added).

Paul plainly stated these must occur before Christ appears and our gathering to Him. Are there Old Testament references for this person? Yes. Daniel 7:24–25,

> And the ten horns out of this kingdom are ten kings that shall arise: and another shall rise after them; and he shall be diverse from the first, and he shall subdue three kings. And he shall speak great words against the most High, and shall wear out the saints of the most High, and think to change times and laws: and they shall be given into his hand until a time and times and the dividing of time.

Daniel 7:21–22 says,

> I beheld, and the same horn made war with the saints, and prevailed against them; Until the Ancient of days came, and judgment was given to the saints of the most High; and the time came that the saints possessed the kingdom.

This same one whom Paul said would debut, will arise as Satan's agent. Daniel noted 'the horn' that made war with the saints until the Ancient of days came is this same emissary. Do we see this horn, this man, revealed by the time John's call up to heaven in Revelation 4:1–2 occurs?

No.

Question: Where in the Bible do we see this one revealed?

The rebellion is occurring over several chapters leading (which in our time has already begun but is not near completion) into chapter 13, and where we see the man of lawlessness exposed is in chapter 13.

In Revelation 13:1–17 (ESV) we read a great description of character traits and actions he will take:

> And I saw a beast rising out of the sea, with ten horns and seven heads, with ten diadems on its horns and blasphemous names on its heads. And the beast that I saw was like a leopard; its feet were like a bear's, and its mouth was like a lion's mouth. And to it the dragon gave his power and his throne and great authority. One of its heads seemed to have a mortal wound, but its mortal wound was healed, and the whole earth marveled as they followed the beast . . . and they worshiped the beast, saying, "Who is like the beast, and who can fight against it?" And the beast was given a mouth uttering haughty and blasphemous words, and it was allowed to exercise authority for forty-two months. It opened its mouth to utter blasphemies against God, blaspheming his name and his dwelling, that is, those who dwell in heaven. Also it was allowed to make war on the saints and to conquer them. And authority was given it over every tribe and people and language and nation, and all who dwell on earth will worship it, everyone whose name has not been written before the foundation of the world in the book of life of the Lamb who was slain. If anyone has an ear, let him hear . . . Here is a call for the endurance and faith of the saints. Then I saw another beast rising out of the earth. It had two horns like a lamb and it spoke like a dragon. It exercises all the authority of the first beast in its presence, and makes the earth and its inhabitants worship the first beast, whose mortal wound was

healed. It performs great signs, even making fire come down from heaven to earth in front of people, and by the signs it is allowed to work in the presence of the beast it deceives those who dwell on earth, telling them to make an image for the beast that was wounded by the sword and yet lived. And it was allowed to give breath to the image of the beast, so that the image of the beast might even speak and might cause those who would not worship the image of the beast to be slain. Also it causes all, both small and great, both rich and poor, both free and slave, to be marked on the right hand or the forehead, so that no one can buy or sell unless he has the mark, that is, the name of the beast or the number of its name.

Second Thess. 2:4–9 (NIV) states,

He will oppose and will exalt himself above all that is called God, or that is worshipped; so that he as God sits in the temple of God, showing himself that he is God. Don't you remember, that, when I was yet with you, I told you these things? And now ye know what is holding him back that he might be revealed in his time. For the secret power of lawlessness is already at work; but the one who now holds it back will continue to do so until he be taken out of the way. And then shall that Wicked be revealed ... Even him, whose coming is by the working of Satan with all power and signs and lying wonders,' – Apostle Paul

Summarizing, when first the rebellion occurs and this wicked one is released during the Tribulation, we can know

Jesus' return and our gathering is nearer—very near in fact. We should look for Him *after* these markers. Since the rebellion doesn't occur and this wicked one isn't let out before Revelation 4:1–2, how could it be said the rapture will occur at Revelation 4:1–2? Regarding His appearing and our gathering, it is still imminent by this point at Revelation 13.

CHAPTER ELEVEN

HOLY SPIRIT AND THE TRIBULATION

B ut what about Christians not being on the Earth during the Tribulation and the Holy Spirit taken out of the world?

Have you heard this before . . . that if the Holy Spirit were removed from the world, then no Christians would be on earth? This notion of the Holy Spirit will be taken out of the world during the Tribulation rests in this one verse. 'For the secret power of lawlessness is already at work; but the one who now holds it back will continue to do so till he is taken out of the way' (2 Thess. 2:7 NIV).

Some Bible versions capitalize the pronoun *he* in this verse. If you read several Bible versions, fine. I do too. Just remember, if that pronoun is capitalized, it's been changed. Some Bible revisers put their spin on verses so it says what they want it to say or to produce a Bible with more modern or cultural verbiage. This pronoun is not capitalized in the Greek text.[1] In a body of writing, capitalizing every pronoun referring to God, from *he* to *He* and from *him* to *Him*, for example, is a modern show of personal respect and honor by many authors though not necessary. It isn't wrong to capitalize, but it is inaccurate when it isn't incontrovertible here whether this *one* is the Holy Spirit. I'm just saying, someone capitalized this pronoun in their Bible version probably because it was their belief the one restraining is the Holy Spirit. I've never known letter capitalization be advised as a hermeneutical 'look for' to exegete Scripture. To capitalize or not is subject to change with literary rules and is not a credible *tell*, especially for trying to prove a stance like this.

Do you see any word in the sentence suggesting the Holy Spirit? I don't either. Nothing here insinuates this one who stands in the way holding back is the Holy Spirit, and there are no other Bible verses to support this. If someone can produce a verse showing such with clarity, I'd certainly be open to see it.

I've read commentary suggesting two alternatives: one, Satan, who might hold back *his* beast until the right time, like a bad dog owner might hold back his dangerous dog until the ready release; or two, that it could be Michael the archangel who is restraining. Revelations 12 tells of a battle in heaven between Michael with his angels against Satan with his, who lose and are evicted. Then we see the following in chapter 13, "that Wicked one" is revealed.

I am inclined to think it is Michael due to Daniel 12, but I can't say with certainty. Nonetheless, this book covers the rapture and not all end-time prophetic pieces, so I will honestly say at this point that I don't know for sure who is restraining. Still, these two possibilities have no bearing on Christians still being present on earth during the tribulation.

Question: If the Holy Spirit supposedly departs out of the world and with Him all Christians, then how will others receive Christ during the Adversity (Tribulation) if none evangelize? It is the Holy Spirit who convicts. But if He weren't present, then no one during the tribulations would be convicted of his or her need for salvation. Who will share the gospel during the tribulations if no one has the Holy Spirit within them, since only Christians have the Holy Spirit within them? *If* there were no Holy Spirit within people during the Tribulation Period, this could mean there would be no Christians on the earth. This would support the pre-trib view . . . but it might not.

Do any verses reveal Christians will be on the earth after chapter 5? Good question. Yes.

Let's look at verses recognizing saints after Revelation 5. First, let's see what Old Testament verses show.

Zephaniah 1:15 described "the day of the LORD", "the day of trouble" and "day of wrath" as a "day of clouds and thick darkness". Then Ezekiel 34:12 stated the LORD will seek and gather His sheep "in the cloudy and dark day." If we recall, Daniel wrote the son of perdition would wear out the saints and make war with them. Daniel 7:24–25,

> . . . And he shall speak great words against the most High, and shall wear out the saints of the most High, and think to change times and laws: and they shall be given into his hand until a time and times and the dividing of time.

Daniel 7:21–22 says "I beheld, and the same horn made war with the saints, and prevailed against them; until the Ancient of days came . . ." How could the saints be worn out and prevailed against if they weren't in the earth? Hmm.

Joel 3:13–16 says,

> "Swing the sickle, for the harvest is ripe . . . Multitudes, multitudes in the valley of decision! For the day of the Lord is near in the valley of decision. The sun and moon will be darkened, and the stars no longer shine . . . But the Lord will be a refuge for His people,"

In Matthew 24:22 and Mark 13:22, Jesus said the days of persecution would be shortened for the elect's sake, meaning the "elect" *will be* present for the days' shortening. We've already discussed who the elect are in chapter six and where they are in position relative to the period of tribulation. Here are passages found in Revelation past chapter 4 referring to saints, the people of God.

> And white robes were given unto every one of them; and it was said unto them, that they should rest yet for a little season, until their fellow servants also and their brethren, that should be killed as they were, should be fulfilled. (Rev. 6:11)

To those saints awaiting their brethren who would be killed, God will give them white robes. Obviously, there are believers who will die which have not yet at this point. Revelation 7:4 says,

> "Do not harm the land or the sea or the trees until we put a seal on the foreheads of the servants of our God." Then I heard the number of those who were sealed: 144,000 from all the tribes of Israel.

These sealed Jewish servants of God will be witnesses on earth. Paul taught the Holy Spirit seals believers (Eph.1:13). Don't you think these servants have the Holy Spirit within them?

Revelation 7:13–14 states,

Then one of the elders asked me, "These in white robes—who are they, and where did they come from?" I answered, "Sir, you know." And he said, "These are they who have come out of the great tribulation; they have washed their robes and made them white in the blood of the Lamb."

Notice these saints came out of the great tribulation. Revelation 12:11, 17 (NIV) says,

They triumphed over him by the blood of the Lamb and by the word of their testimony; they did not love their lives so much as to shrink from death ... Then the dragon was enraged at the woman and went off to wage war against the rest of her offspring—those who keep God's commands and hold fast their testimony about Jesus.

In these two verses, who overcame by the blood of the Lamb and the word of their testimony, which keep God's commands and hold fast to their testimony? Saints. Who else partakes in the blood of the Lamb? Saints.

In Revelation 13:7, 10 it says,

It was given power to wage war against God's holy people and to conquer them. And it was given authority

over every tribe, people, language and nation . . . This
calls for patient endurance and faithfulness on the part
of God's people [saints].

Why would saints need endurance and faithfulness if
not on earth facing trials? Rev.14:12 says, 'This calls for
patient endurance on the part of the people of God who
keep his commands and remain faithful to Jesus.' Of whom
does this call for patience and endurance? —the people of
God who must have the Holy Spirit. One more verse; Revelation 14:13 (NIV),

Then I heard a voice from heaven say, "Write this:
Blessed are the dead who die in the Lord from now on."
"Yes" says the Spirit, "they will rest from their labor, for
their deeds will follow them."

Who is it that dies 'in the Lord' *from this point on*? Hmm.

We have a verse this far into Revelation straightfor-
wardly stating that, from this point forward, those who die
in the Lord will be blessed. Who else can 'die in the Lord' but
a believer?

From these verses, how can it be said the Holy Spirit,
and thus believers, will be taken out of the world during the
tribulation? It can't be.

The Holy Spirit brooded over the earth at creation
before there were any believers on the earth. He worked in
the world, coming upon and departing from people in the
Old Testament, before He ever abode within any following
the Cross. This explains He has worked in the world before
there were any indwelt believers. There's no reason then to
imagine He can't work with people in a world absent of

believers. So then, the idea 'if God took Christians out of the world, then the Holy Spirit must be gone out of the world too' isn't congruent. The relation between the two doesn't altogether functionally agree. Furthermore, if the Holy Spirit were the one holding back at this point in the Tribulation, how can He be since He is already taken out of the world by Revelation 4 in the pre-tribulation rapture view? If one believes Revelation 4:1–2 is the rapture, then one must believe the Tribulation began before Revelation 4:1–2, according to Paul in Second Thessalonians 2:1–3. By the Tribulation in Revelation, there shouldn't be any believers (but there are) and the Holy Spirit shouldn't be present holding back in the Tribulation up to chapter thirteen, according to the pre-trib notion. Therefore, it makes little sense that the Holy Spirit is the one holding back, *especially* with a pre-trib rapture view.

For argument's sake, let's say this one described holding back in Second Thessalonians is the Holy Spirit. Nothing in the verses indicates this one will be *taken out* of the world. It says the one (or he) will be taken *out of the way* (or out of the *midst*, Gk.)—not *out of the world*. And additionally, in other Bible versions where it says the *one who restrains stops restraining* doesn't translate to mean "taken out of the world".

Still, all the details Jesus and Paul prophesied must fall in sequence and must agree in all parts, regardless of anyone's view. To say these saints mentioned from chapter 6 through chapter 14 are only the 144,000 Jews is not really supported from what is read. If they are, they still should have the Holy Spirit within them, right? The premise that the Holy Spirit is removed out of the world while believers are still on earth contradicts its own assertion.

Not all the predicted details, which will happen first and by the rapture, will have occurred by Revelation 13. With the verses seen by this point in Revelation, it is obvious Christians are still on earth, and thus, the Holy Spirit is within them as well.

CHAPTER TWELVE

THE GATHERING

Everyone wants to know when the rapture will happen. We're about to get to it. Let's recap. Jesus, whose words are true, said there would be signs in the heavens that would precede His return: the sun will darken, the moon turns the color of blood, stars will fall from the heavens. These signs were found in Revelation chapters 6 through 8. He said the days would be shortened for the sake of the elect, meaning believers would still exist on earth during the Tribulation, thus the Holy Spirit is not removed. Jesus said there would be a trumpet sound. Apostle Paul said it would be the last trumpet sound. The significant seventh and last trumpet is found in chapter 11:15, as we read. In Second Thessalonians 2:1–3, Paul said there would be a defiance against God and everything godly, and the man of perdition would be uncovered before Christ returns and the church is gathered. We find the rebellion building up into chapter 13 and the man of lawlessness revealed occurring in chapter 13. Therefore, according to what Paul wrote, the rapture has

to be after chapter 13. Thus far, all the descriptors Jesus
told in the Gospels of Matthew, Mark and Luke, and
disclosed by Paul in First Corinthians 15, First Thessalonians 4:14–18, and Second Thessalonians 2:1–3 fits in
sequence, just as they said, in the chapters of Revelation
we have covered.

Now, at this point in our search, what's left from Jesus'
and Paul's detail that we haven't encountered yet in Revelation is Jesus descending and appearing in the clouds and
the air, an angel shouting, and the saints' rapture. When we
find these last three together, we have found the rapture
event. So where is it?

GATHERING AND HARVEST

Before I reveal that passage, I'd like to refer to a few verses
about the harvest because Jesus often referred to people as
wheat, fruit, and a field of harvest. He used this common
agricultural expression with His disciples and people of the
day for illustrating the Kingdom. You'll see soon why this
image is key to recognizing the rapture event in Revelation.
Let's validate this illustration with a few verses. Matthew
9:37–38 says,

> Then he said to his disciples, "The harvest is plentiful but
> the workers are few. Ask the Lord of the harvest, there-
> fore, to send out workers into his harvest field."

Matthew 13:30 says,

> Jesus said "Let both grow together until the harvest. At
> that time I will tell the harvesters: First collect the weeds

and tie them in bundles to be burned; then gather the wheat and bring it into my barn."

In Luke 10:2 it says, "He told them, 'The harvest is plentiful, but the workers are few. Ask the Lord of the harvest, therefore, to send out workers into his harvest field.'"

In John 4:35 Jesus said, "Don't you have a saying, 'It's still four months until harvest'? I tell you, open your eyes and look at the fields! They are ripe for harvest.'" In John 15:1, Jesus said, "I am the true vine, and my Father is the gardener."

First Corinthians 3:7–8 states,

So neither the one who plants nor the one who waters is anything, but only God, who makes things grow. The one who plants and the one who waters have one purpose, and they will each be rewarded according to their own labor. For we are co-workers in God's service; you are God's field, God's building.

We find in James 5:7,

Be patient therefore, brethren, unto the coming of the Lord. Behold, the husbandman waits for the precious fruit of the earth, and has long patience for it, until he receive the early and latter rain.

Apparently, Jesus compared people to a harvest. This is important now in understanding why He compared people to harvests and harvesting. He not only used this illustration because Israel's society at the time was widely agrarian and He wanted to connect with people, but also because it would help them understand the rapture. For Jesus, the harvest description is not metaphor only, but is also literal. Paul understood the literal metaphor of harvest/harvesting being made was synonymous with and setting the stage as the description of the rapture. We find it used later in Revelation, in which he called it "our gathering" in Second Thessalonians 2:1, as in gathering sheaves of wheat, a metaphor for God's people.

The next passage discloses when the rapture happens in Revelation. Readers typically run past this passage in oversight. My guess is some do because it nullifies the pretrib view or because another harvest takes place right after it.

Now, the verses you've been waiting for, found in Revelation 14:14–16 (NIV), that pinpoint the rapture.

> I looked, and there before me was a white cloud, and seated on the cloud was one like a son of man [in KJV, the Son of Man] with a crown of gold on his head and a sharp sickle in his hand. Then another angel came out of the temple and called in a loud voice to him who was sitting on the cloud, "Take your sickle and reap, because the time to reap has come, for the harvest of the earth is ripe." So he [Jesus] who was seated on the cloud swung his sickle over the earth, and the earth was harvested.

Doesn't this describe the rapture, a gathering in? Yes. Are all the remaining three elements that Jesus described in Matthew 24, Mark 13 and Luke 21 found here? Yes.

Are the details Paul described in 1 Thess. 4:14–18 shown here? Yes.

Does Jesus appear in the clouds? Yes, He, the Son of Man, appears sitting on a white cloud.

Does an angel loudly shout? Yes. He isn't commanding Jesus to thrust His sickle to reap, but announcing it is time to do it.

Is there a description of God's people being gathered up as a harvest of people? Yes, it is here. This is the rapture. Who will do the reaping? Jesus. He is holding the sickle. Notice the Bible states the "harvest of the earth is ripe."

Harvesting is performed when the plant food is ripe, so timing is important. Every fruit ripens in its time. In gathering produce at the wrong time, one might end up damaging the true essence of the fruit, and insult the forces of nature that came together to nurture it and bring out its best flavors. Reaping and harvest can be metaphors, but for Jesus, they are also literal because He has the power to harvest and reap people, and this matches Paul and Jesus' details accurately. Nowhere else in Revelation do we see harvesting. Our attentions should be cued to this passage for this reason alone. The last and all three descriptive elements pertaining to the rapture crest right here in Revelation 14:14–16. No other places in Revelation are these elements found. This is it. It is undeniable. These are the verses we have been looking for, and it is what we wait for —our gathering —our rapture. This is our homecoming— oh blessed day! And they match Jesus' own prophetic testimony. We must believe Jesus' own words regarding His return, quoted from the gospel passages. This is when the momentous fulfillment of the mystery of God, aforementioned in Revelation 10:7, happens. It occurs where it occurs in God's Word without respect to any view. Let where the rapture is found form your view, and let the view fit where it is found. (See the chart of sequences fulfilled at chapter end.)

To add to this book the affirming opinion of other persons, there is no need—Scripture is enough. Again, compare it to Jesus' words from Matthew 24:30–31,

> Then will appear the sign of the Son of Man in heaven . . .
> when they see the Son of Man coming on the clouds of
> heaven, with power and great glory. And he will send his
> angels with a loud trumpet call, and they will gather his
> elect from the four winds, from one end of the heavens to
> the other.

The two passages match. Beloved, this is the blessed hope God's Word spoke of! And it is plain to see.

UNDERSTANDING 'THE DAY OF THE LORD' WITH PARADOX

Now that we can see what Paul said in Second Thessalonians 2:1–3 would happen in sequence, happened in order at Revelation 13–14:16, I'd like to refer back to Second Thessalonians 2:3,

> Don't let anyone deceive you in any way, for that day
> will not come until the rebellion occurs and the man of
> lawlessness is revealed, the man doomed to
> destruction.

In Paul's words, *that day* referred to Christ's coming and our gathering (2 Thess. 2:1). We've learned earlier, *day* can mean a day, a period of time, a time or an age. We can see

Christ's second coming began with His appearing beginning in Revelation 14:1,

> Then I looked, and there before me was the Lamb, standing on Mount Zion, and with him 144,000 who had his name and his Father's name written on their foreheads.

Here in Revelation 14:1 is the beginning of the period or time of His appearance, which continues where He is seen again in verses 14–16 where the rapture occurs. This reference and time period in 14:1–16 are part of that day, marking the beginning of His coming and our gathering Paul referred to in Second Thessalonians 2:1. Whether what happens in Revelation chapter 14 does so in a twenty-four-hour day or over a small time period we can't be exactly sure. I think it's very short because from verse 2 to 13 are proclamations with no actions taking place and no relation to earthly time. But the description still fits Paul's reference and definition of *that day*. I believe *that day*, 'the day of the Lord', is a single day *and* a measure of time beginning from Revelation 14:1 through the Tribulation end into the millennium.

This is no conflict saying 'the day of the Lord' is both a single day and a period of time. It is not a contradiction, but rather a paradox. Let me help you understand what I mean by defining paradox. A paradox is a statement, situation or belief where two or more things seem absurd and to contradict the other(s) but do not, and are actually true and possible together. It is two or more conflicting ideas contained in the same truth.

In Charles Dickens' classic *A Tale of Two Cities*, the first line in the first chapter is a paradoxical statement, "It was the best of times, it was the worst of times, it was an age of wisdom, it was an age of foolishness."[1] How could it be the best of times and the worst of times at the same time? In 19th century industrial England, it was the worst of times for low-class men, women and children who worked long hours like slaves for pennies in factories, but it was the best of times for the factory owners who became very rich.

Understanding the Three Person Godhead: the co-existence of the Father, Son and Holy Spirit in One God is not a contradiction but a paradox. Jesus taught paradoxes: the last will be first and the first will be last; you have to die to live; you have to give to receive.

Another case is salvation. Do people have free will to choose, or is it election? I don't believe it is only one *or* the other; but it is both—one *and* the other, because Scripture supports that both God chooses *and* He lets people choose.

The Church is a paradox. It's a Building and a Body. A building is a rigid, inflexible, immovable structure while a body is elastic, moving, and continually changing. What seems like many contradictions by King Solomon in Ecclesiastes are really paradoxes.

God's wisdom and understanding of His own ways and plans are higher and deeper than our understanding of them. Understanding paradox helps us to better understand His ways and His word, like "the day of the Lord." This paradox, "the day of the Lord," broadly describes the period of Jesus' coming from His first appearance at Revelation 14:1, including the day of the rapture in 14:14–16, through to Armageddon and up into the millennium. All of this qualifies as "the day of the Lord." This is the day that the LORD has made, I will rejoice and be glad in it.

I prefer to not ascribe to this or that rapture-tribulation position. It isn't exactly in the middle of the Tribulation or exactly at the end, but it definitely isn't before the Tribulation. I don't care to label a view or stance to it. Really, why do that? Label it whatever you want or just forget labels altogether. Labels cause people to debate their position instead of being impartial with God's Word. This should not divide us, Beloved. We shouldn't become ireful over this. It should unite us so we might encourage one another. But knowing when it happens in Revelation is important. You can see that I have only directed you to God's Word, letting it plainly say what it says. I didn't allegorize or use any ambiguous verses that say nothing about the rapture or its position to the Tribulation, or that could easily be misinterpreted. This rapture is where our hope in seeing Him lies. We need to understand and acknowledge when it occurs in Revelation so we will be established and not alarmed like Paul affirmed.

HOW WILL WE BE TAKEN?

How will we be taken up? Is He going to 'beam us up'? Will God teleport us somehow? Or will it just be some forever unexplainable, supernatural miracle God does but reveals later? Let's see what Jesus said.

> And he will send his angels with a loud trumpet call, and they will gather his elect from the four winds, from one end of the heavens to the other." (Matthew 24:31)

Matthew 13:39 says, " . . . and the enemy who sows

them is the devil. The harvest is the end of the age, and *the harvesters are angels.*"

You read it. He will send His angels to grab us in the blink of an eye, the speed of light. BLINK—we're in the clouds and the air looking at Jesus. How completely amazing will that be? And He will change our bodies from corruptible to incorruptible ones in that instantaneous transition, somehow by His amazingly great power! Everything God has planned for us in this will be beyond comprehension. He will out-do anything we could imagine. We need to get ready.

It is uncertain if there will be piles of clothes left behind on the floor wherever every believer would have been at that moment. I just know we who believe in the true Jesus Christ will be gone. "Two men will be in the field; one will be taken and the other left. Two women will be grinding with a hand mill; one will be taken the other left" (Matthew 24:40–41). People will do the normal variety of activities and suddenly. The believer will disappear and the unbeliever will be left dazed and fearful. We can only imagine the news stories told as millions of disappearances and missing persons reports will flood the airwaves, digital media and internet. Jesus said in Luke 21:26–28,

Men's hearts failing them for fear, and for looking after those things which are coming on the earth: for the powers of heaven shall be shaken. And then shall they see the Son of man coming in a cloud with power and great glory. And when these things begin to come to pass, then look up, and lift up your heads; for your redemption draws nigh.

Amen, Lord Jesus. Let it be unto us, your servants, as You have said.

In summary, we can see unmistakably that Revelation 14:14–16 positions the rapture. Understanding paradox helps to understand better the "day of the Lord." In light of all we have covered so far, how can be it misunderstood any longer that the rapture occurs before the Tribulation? When you read further to the end of Section Two, you will understand better.

PROPHETIC SEQUENTIAL SIGNS PERTAINING TO THE CHRIST'S RETURN & THE RAPTURE

	Predicted	Fulfilled
Celestial signs	Matt. 24:29 Mark 13:24–25 Luke 21:25–26	Rev. 6:12–13
Last Trumpet Sounds	Matt. 24:31 1Cor.15:52 1Thess. 4: 16	Rev. 11:15
Falling Away/ Rebellion	2Thess. 2:3	Rev. 13 (actually begins before the Tribulation and reaches fullness by Rev. 13)
Man of lawlessness revealed	2 Thess. 2:1–3	Rev. 13
See Christ in the clouds & <u>air</u>, angelic shout, elect/ saints gathered	Matt.24:30–31 Mark 13:26–27 Luke 21:27 1Thess. 4:16–17	Rev.14:14–16
God's wrath after rapture	1Thess.1:10 1Thess. 5:9 Rev. 3:10	Rev.16:1–18:17 Rev. 19:15–18

CHAPTER THIRTEEN

SAVED FROM THE HOUR

What about "saved from the hour"? We have looked at markers preceding the rapture to help find its placement. Now, let's look at a marker we know will follow it. This will solidify the rapture's position further by sandwiching it between events Scripture says will happen before *and* after it in the course of the chapters and verses of Revelation. So, let's look at this marker, which follows the rapture.

> To the church at Philadelphia, "Since you have kept my command to endure patiently, I will also keep you from the hour of trial that is going to come on the whole world to test the inhabitants of the earth." (Rev. 3:10)

The marker after the rapture is "the hour of wrath." So, the *keeping from the hour* didn't happen yet. Revelation 3:10 is an early prophetic word, which includes a prophetic word, that will occur later in Revelation, and further in the future than where we are now. What Jesus prophesied to John recorded in 3:10 plays out, starting in Chapter 15 continuing through Chapter 18. This needs to be understood; not all things written by John in Revelation, as given to him, occur in chronological order from beginning to end from chapter one through chapter twenty-two, and at some points there is a little overlap. This takes careful reading comprehension of the many visions and imagery shown to Apostle John.

> He said in a loud voice, "Fear God and give him glory, because the hour of his judgment has come [is coming]. Worship him who made the heavens, the earth, the sea and the springs of water." (Rev. 14:7)

This is the hour Revelation 3:10 spoke of. Here the angel declares aloud the hour of the LORD's judgment (or wrath) is coming upon the earth, the beast and Babylon. This verse declares the coming hour God saves His people from experiencing, but it won't manifest yet in Revelation until chapter 16.

Jesus cited Noah's experience of the Great Flood when referring to the rapture, the tribulation and His judgment. When Noah and his family entered the ark, they were sealed in and protected from the judgment that came quickly upon the earth. I believe the ark being raised "high above the earth" is a picture of the rapture of saints, escaping the wrath of God's judgment (Gen. 7:17 ESV). Ezekiel 34:12b through 13a says God will gather His sheep out of countries on "in the dark and cloudy day". Zephaniah wrote that those who seek righteousness, meekness and humility might be hidden from the day of the Lord's wrath (Zeph. 2:3b). Saints disappearing in rapture from the earth is the 'hiding', the protecting.

Again, what do we see prior to chapter 16 in Revelation 14:14–16? The Son of Man sitting on a cloud, wearing a crown and having a sickle in His hand. What's a sickle for? Harvesting. An angel shouts. The earth is reaped, saving the saints from the hour of wrath, just as the Bible said. An angel announces the hour is coming but is not yet (14:7), then the Lord raptures His people (Rev. 14:14–16) before the hour and wrath of God (Rev. 16), just as He promised. The marker of His wrath follows the rapture; hence, wherever this maker occurs, the rapture must be before it. According to sequential events, His coming and rapture is between the rebellion and the revealing of the antichrist *and* the hour of wrath.

WHEN THE WRATH OF GOD AND THE HOUR OF TRIAL BEGINS

Another angel came out of the temple in heaven, and he too had a sharp sickle. Still another angel, who had charge of the fire, came from the altar and called in a loud voice to him who had the sharp sickle, "Take your sharp sickle and gather the clusters of grapes from the earth's vine, because its grapes are ripe." The angel swung his sickle on the earth, gathered its grapes and threw them into the great winepress of God's wrath. (Rev. 14:17–20 [NIV])

Please notice in this passage, it isn't Jesus holding the sickle this time, but an angel. Let's recall Matthew 13:39 " The harvest is the end of the age, and the harvesters are angels." Jesus said angels are the harvesters, plural. Yes, when Jesus reaps, they will gather up the saints. But next, angels will harvest the unsaved in Revelation 14:17–20.

'Fully ripe grapes' is used to describe the generations of peoples in the earth that are unsaved by this point in the Tribulation. Also, look where these grapes (unsaved people) will be thrown . . . into the winepress of God's wrath.

But why? Ripe grapes are good.

Yes, but these "grapes" are *fully* ripe. Grapes left on the vine's branches won't continue to grow and look pretty as long as you leave them. They will fully ripen and fall off the branch. This is when fruit loses its beautiful color, browns, softens and becomes mushy. We normally discard fruit at this stage. This is when fruit is fully ripe. What we call spoiled, overripe, rotten, or *gone bad* is actually fully ripe fruit. That's the picture here—fruit that stayed on the branch much too long, was not picked, has fallen off, and totally unable to be connected to the life source again. That's the image here . . . people who will wait too long, will become totally depraved (fully ripe) and never get connected nor can they connect themselves by this point to the Life Source, Jesus Christ. The opportunity to be saved has ended. This is where Jeremiah's prophecy (one of the saddest verses in the Bible to me) comes true, "The harvest is past, the summer is ended, and we are not saved" (Jer. 8:20). This is why the harvest of verse 17–19 is not saints, contrasted to verses 14–16. They were recorded together in John's vision but they won't occur in time together.

(If by this point you are unsure of your place, of which harvest you will be a part, see the APPENDIX for a prayer you can pray to be saved.)

PERSPECTIVES ON TWO HARVESTS

Perspective is all about the view. On the ground, you can see what happens on the closer, detailed scale person to person: the cars next to you on the road, every little thing around you, etc. However, flying in a plane high above the ground provides a unique view. As the aircraft rises higher, you can't see the smaller detail you may want and once saw. You get a view on the larger, broader scale of traffic flow, what a city looks like from above, and you can appreciate better its relation, size and proximity to another town. Revelation 14:14–20 contrasts from a high level the scene of two occurrences; the day of the Lord's rapture occurring in verses 14–16 as we have already discussed, and the foreshadowed day of the Lord's wrath in Revelation 14:17–20. These verses are a broad description of God's wrath from a high perspective, condensing chapters 15 through 18 with a beginning-to-end, metaphorical-literal glimpse, foreshadowing what will come in the next two to three chapters.

The Bible denotes a great tribulation, that last part of the Adversities, as worse than the first half, with no saints mentioned any further in Revelation through the end of the Tribulation. First Thessalonians 5:9 says, "For God did not appoint us to suffer wrath but to receive salvation through our Lord Jesus Christ." Paul said we are not scheduled an appointment to experience as innocent victims, God's wrath. The imputed righteousness of Jesus, received by grace through faith, sets any free from this appointment.

Not all of the persecution period is His wrath, but it is undeniable that the verses 18 through 20 speak of wrath not previously discharged in Revelation.

In chapter 16, the wrath of God will be intense. Not only will it include all the previous trials of the beginning of sorrows, the increased labor and the hard labor pangs of the Tribulation leading up to the rapture but wrath will compound the miseries. The vials of wrath are prepared and will be announced when chapter 15 unfolds in time. Chapter 16 is when His wrath will be poured out. This is what we will escape by the rapture, which again occurs beforehand in Revelation 14:14–16. In Revelation 16:1, John said, 'Then I heard a loud voice from the temple saying to the seven angels, "Go, pour out the seven bowls of God's wrath on the earth." Wrath will be discharged as each vial of the seven plagues materializes. This is when the wrath of God begins and continues into chapter 18. This is the hour saints are saved from, not the whole tribulation, but from this part. "Terrified at her torment, they will stand far off and cry: 'Woe! Woe to you, great city, you mighty city of Babylon! In one *hour* your doom has come!'" (Rev. 18:10).

So then, the two harvests witnessed by John happened in a sequence; therefore he recorded them this way. The harvest of saints happens in Revelation 14:14-16 before the next foreshadowed harvest in verses 17-19.

'In one hour such great wealth has been brought to ruin!' "Every sea captain, and all who travel by ship, the sailors, and all who earn their living from the sea, will stand far off.'" (Rev. 18:17 NIV).

Since Scripture specifies the last trumpet sound, the apostasy and the revealing of the Antichrist will occur before the rapture, and the hour of wrath would follow after the rapture; then, the rapture must occur after chapter 13 but before chapter 16. Accordingly, saints will be kept from wrath as God promised and determined.

PART TWO

CHAPTER FOURTEEN

ARGUMENTS AGAINST A VIEW

M y intent in this section is not to answer every argument by every author or person with an opinion towards the pre-trib rapture view, but only to address a few of the more common objections heard through the years, with one in particular near this section's end, which I recently found surprising myself—I expect you will, too.

WHAT ABOUT IMMINENCY?

Imminency is a particular hallmark associated with Jesus' return. It is the idea that Jesus can return at any time. Some believers think imminency is only a pre-trib view expectation. All rapture views agree with imminency. All believers expect Jesus' return is imminent, but some of us have a different idea what that means. You won't find the word *imminent* in the Bible either, like the word *rapture*, but without question, it is expressed.

What does imminent mean? *Collin's English Dictionary*

defines imminent as: forthcoming, immediate, inevitable, unavoidable, impending, looming.[1] Jesus already came once in the life He lived on the earth as a man, born of the virgin, Mary. It is prophesied He will come again gathering His people and ushering in His Kingdom's rule on earth, conquering all dark foes once and for all. His return is nearer than ever.

Verses do actually say to watch and pray, for you don't know what day or hour He comes . . . that He will come like a thief in the night when you don't expect. Look at what Jesus said in the following three passages: Jesus stated in Matthew 24:42, 44 "Watch therefore: for ye know not what hour your Lord doth come . . . Therefore, be ye also ready: for in such an hour as ye think not the Son of man cometh." In Matthew 25:13 He said, "Watch therefore, for ye know neither the day nor the hour wherein the Son of man comes." and in Mark 13:33 "Take ye heed, watch and pray: for ye know not when the time is." See, there is a time.

Revelation 3:3 Jesus said, "Remember, therefore, what you have received and heard; hold it fast and repent. But if you do not wake up, I will come like a thief, and you will not know at what time I will come to you."

What these verses tell us is Jesus said it wouldn't be known exactly when His return will be. These mean His return will be unknown and unexpected. An unknown date of return doesn't automatically mean one's return can be *any time*, nor does an unexpected return mean this. No verse actually says He can return any time. Regarding Jesus' return, some writers think imminent means He can come *any time*, but biblical literature doesn't communicate this. Definitions for imminent do not connote *any time*, but *definitely coming and coming soon*. Jesus strenuously asserted in

Revelation 22:20 He would come quickly, but that doesn't mean *any time*. For the verse "Watch therefore, for you know not what hour your Lord is coming," (Matt. 24:42) says we won't know when. This does not mean any time. And "Be ready, for the Son of Man is coming at an hour when you do not expect him", (Matt. 24:44) says His coming is unexpected. Unexpected does not mean 'any time' either.

One author purports that the Early Church expected Jesus to come at any time. I have seen no verses supporting He could come any time, but it can be understood they believed it was forthcoming, immediate, inevitable, unavoidable, impending, or unexpected. If I were alive then and I heard Jesus say this generation would not pass away before He returned, I would think He would return any time during my lifetime, too. We know, looking back, Jesus didn't mean the earthly-age generation He was born into was the world's final generation. During the Early Church years, saints may have believed Jesus could come at any time, but they would also have had to believe the preceding details Jesus and Paul described would therefore have to occur any time, too.

By the 'last days' depiction told by Jesus, it is easy to understand why they thought He would return soon in their lifetime. Some of the 'end times' details were occur-ring during their years: wars, famines, persecutions, false teachers and phony Christs, etc. No wonder His return was assumed to be quite near. Still, there were details Jesus and Paul gave which hadn't happened yet, but there's no reason those details couldn't occur any moment in their lifetime, with the rapture ensuing well before our generation, except by God's timing.

Prophetic timing and prophecy fulfillment are familiar concepts. Christ's birth and death fulfilled many Old Testament prophecies. Prophecies must be fulfilled in their timing; like when He came the first time, before He went to the cross, and before the Holy Spirit's baptism occurred at Pentecoste, just to name a few. Paul stated in Romans 5:6, *at the right time,* Christ died for the ungodly; and 'when *the set time had fully come,* God sent his Son,' (Gal. 4:4 NIV). Some prophetic events have a sequential order for fulfillment, like His return being assigned a specific time and sequence, which only the Father knows.

Jesus and Paul indicated markers that must occur before He returns and raptures His elect. Although we know these markers, we still may not know exactly when He is coming. I wonder if these signs are ignored because they disprove the pre-trib definition of imminent? Paul said in Second Thessalonians 2:1–3 the rebellion and the revelation of the man of lawlessness must happen first before Jesus returns and gathers us up.

Knowing these happen beforehand doesn't mean the day or hour is known. It just means those markers can happen any time, too, according to timing and scriptural sequence. Even after these, there is still an unknown time elapse before Jesus appears on the cloud; therefore, we still won't know exactly when to expect Him. So, saying Christ could come any time is true, yet it isn't. It could happen any time, as long as all the markers predicted occur accordingly and sequentially. But until they transpire, He won't return because every jot and tittle must come to pass. Considering, I don't see how His return could be at any moment yet. In conclusion, Scripture doesn't agree with the pre-trib characterization that Christ's return can happen at any time, unless all the sequential pre-occurring events foretold do first.

NO PRE-TRIB RAPTURE MARKERS?

God is always previous. He knows the future. He is a God who wants to be our Guide. Amos 3:6 says, 'the LORD God does nothing without first revealing it to his prophets.' How many times did He say in the Bible that He will guide and speak before we ask, that He will make a way in the wilderness? He is God of the Way; a God who gives directions, telling His people what to look for. One pre-trib author said there are no pre-rapture signs thus Christ can come any time.[2]

Considering all the pre-rapture details Jesus and Paul gave, how could it be said there are no pre-rapture markers? How can those details be ignored? Jesus told the crowd, and I paraphrase, *You can tell when it's going to rain or storm by the signs; when the sky is red, or if the wind comes from this direction or that one . . . you know what the weather will be. Why can't you discern the signs of the times?* (Matt.16:2–3). He has provided undeniable pre-rapture harbingers we can't help but notice. Why would He provide them? So we could know them and not miss them; so we can have hope and recognize His nearness. We should be a people, like the men of Issachar, who discern the times and know what to do (1 Chron. 12:32). If one thinks there are no pre-rapture signs, then they won't look for any harbinger cueing His ever-nearness. The thought of the mind will be *why look if there are no signs showing His nearness? If there are no signs and nothing to look for, then I won't be able to tell; so why look for Him? When He comes, He'll get me. Meh, I won't concern myself.* This 'no pre-trib rapture markers' idea, I think, is the mindset of some believers today. A lot of Christians aren't looking for Him; they're just expecting to be taken. But He wants us to concern ourselves and watch. He said so. By this, we know Jesus advocates we notice the signs. "When these things begin to take place, stand up and lift up your heads, because your redemption is drawing near" (Luke 21:27–28).

The previous pre-trib author I read from, LaHaye, dissuaded believers from looking for the signs Jesus said would occur, saying believers shouldn't look for signs instead of watching for Him personally.[3] Why? Looking for and recognizing the signs does not take away from watching for Jesus to appear. Actually, they increase our attention to watch for Him. With the effects from this pandemic (Jesus said there will be pestilences in the last days), people searched to know how very near His coming is. Social media was ablaze with such chat. More pastors, preachers and prophets have spoken more about Jesus' return since this virus outbreak than in the previous ten to twenty years combined. So then, seeing signs makes our *Jesus is coming* antennae go up. God meant for signs to step up our watchfulness. I think interest in markers that pique our interests in Jesus' return are healthy, and so looking for them isn't wrong to do.

JESUS WOULDN'T BEAT HIS BRIDE!

Jesus wouldn't beat His Bride! Ever hear this, as a reason the rapture must be pre-trib? It's so preposterous. Of course, He wouldn't beat His Bride. This statement insinuates that if Jesus allows believers to experience the Tribulation, then

He is guilty of spousal abuse. How preposterous! Why would anyone insinuate such a thing? This implies God wouldn't let any of His saints undergo the persecution since He loves them, but that if He did, its anger and wrath towards them. What? There must be a lack of scriptural knowledge and a misunderstanding of His ways. Here are reasons this is nonsensical.

One, it's against His nature. Jesus won't cause the evil that will come upon the earth to people. That contradicts His character and nature. Obviously, it originates from Satan, his evil scheme and all those spirits of darkness he organizes; however, it is factored into God's plan in what He allows and what He will do.

Two, God did not always keep trials and sufferings from His people. The implication that Noah and his family escaped the flood, and Lot and his family escaped Sodom because they were the righteous living in ungodly societies, as some kind of proof that God will rapture the righteous Church out of the world before the trouble begins, isn't certified scripturally. Yes, these families evaded judgment by God's grace, but they weren't raptured. In many Old Testament instances, the righteous didn't escape experiencing troubles, but became the remnant. There, we can read how God allowed His people of Israel to fall into the suffering and bondage as punishment, which came through other conquering countries like Egypt, Midian, Babylon, and Assyria. Certainly, their sufferings were terrible. God's discipline doesn't mean He wanted to abuse them. The writer of Hebrews wrote the Father disciplines those He loves.

How many times have Christians experienced beatings, sufferings, grief, chastisements, persecutions and death in the world since the Early Church days? Millions. You can read John Foxe's book on Christian martyrdom. It records atrocities and terrible treatments of Christians beginning from the twelve apostles into the Middle Ages. In this present modern day, it is estimated over one hundred thousand Christians per year are persecuted and martyred around the world for their faith.

Consider what Paul and other believers suffered for Christ in these verses. It's amazing what he and those with him went through. 'We are troubled on every side, yet not distressed; we are perplexed, but not in despair; Persecuted, but not forsaken; cast down, but not destroyed;' (2 Cor. 4:8–9).

Are they servants of Christ? (I am out of my mind to talk like this.) I am more. I have worked much harder, been in prison more frequently, been flogged more severely, and been exposed to death again and again. Five times I received from the Jews the forty lashes minus one. Three times I was beaten with rods, once I was pelted with stones, three times I was shipwrecked, I spent a night and a day in the open sea, I have been constantly on the move. I have been in danger from rivers, in danger from bandits, in danger from my fellow Jews, in danger from Gentiles; in danger in the city, in danger in the country, in danger at sea; and in danger from false believers. I have labored and toiled and have often gone without sleep; I have known hunger and thirst and have often gone without food; I have been cold and naked (2 Cor. 11:25–28);

And Second Thessalonians 1:4: 'Therefore, among God's

churches we boast about your perseverance and faith in all the persecutions and trials you are enduring.' also Hebrews 11:36–38,

> Some faced jeers and flogging, and even chains and imprisonment. They were put to death by stoning; they were sawed in two; they were killed by the sword. They went about in sheepskins and goatskins, destitute, persecuted and mistreated—the world was not worthy of them. They wandered in deserts and mountains, living in caves and in holes in the ground.

What does this idea say about God's love towards tortured Christians who were persecuted, burned at the stake, cut in pieces, etc., and experienced all manner of barbarity through the last two thousand years to present? What is implied when God didn't stop over six million Jews from being killed by Hitler's regime? That He abused His own chosen nation of people? Certainly not! If the premise is *because God is good, He would not put Christians through the Tribulation,* then how is the paradox of God's protection and suffering throughout history explained? It is an indictment against His love and judgment. Will anyone rail God is a masochist, that He is unfair? This notion is an extension of the 'Why does God let bad things happen to good people?' question, except in this case, it applies to this future event. This idea is weak and fosters human sympathy, earthly understanding, and rejects the high wisdom and reason of God. God is not bipolar with His love, dearly Beloved—loving one season then pendulum swinging to abuse His Bride in another. No, He dearly loves and cares for His people from beginning to end.

He isn't interested in satisfying every notion of our intellect, reason, or sympathy. He is most interested in satisfying His word, His purposes, and promises. The supposition that saints will be raptured is because God doesn't want us to go through the 'bad stuff'. The Church will be raptured because it is time; time for the mystery of God to be fulfilled, time for the Bride's preparation for marriage.

Not fully understanding and agreeing with every detail of His plan does not mean He is regulated to how we think and feel. Does this mean if God doesn't stop these, He is guilty of abusing His sons and daughters? Absolutely not! Just because terrible things happen doesn't mean He doesn't love and care for those who endure such. What God allows through His permission, He could easily prevent by His power. Romans 8:28 promises He will make all things work together for good for those who love Him and are called according to His purpose. This means whatever He allows, there is a reason, and an upgrade in Christlikeness for us when we respond properly in the situation. Notwithstanding, the scripture doesn't say He would save us from all the tribulation but that He will keep us from— protect us from—deliver us from wrath. First Thessalonians 1:10 says, 'And to wait for his Son from heaven, whom he raised from the dead, even Jesus, which delivered us from the wrath to come.' Yes, the trials will be difficult, but He will save us from wrath. I think *factoring out* suffering from the Christian experience leads to a kind of pre-trib view. We are called to suffer. Peter said so (1 Peter 4:13–19). I don't search for an opportunity to suffer, and we shouldn't do so. We don't have to. If we are obedient to God, it's going to happen. Nevertheless, we need to realize suffering responsively makes us more like Jesus. Remember this, Jesus took upon Himself and endured the judgment and wrath of God for us. I believe what He suffered and bore in His body on the cross was worse than whatever will be suffered during the Tribulation. By bearing sin on the cross, God forsook Jesus for a time. This was the worst of His sufferings. And because He overcame the world and lives in us, then we can too. For us, we will never be forsaken. He humbled and suffered the most and so He was given the most authority (Phil. 2:8–9). Jesus suffered so good would come to us; therefore we may be called to share in His suffering so good will come to others. By this we grow in intimacy, sympathizing and empathizing with Him. Greater authority comes by greater intimacy to Jesus. Don't be surprised to see believers act with more authority in the last days. This is what Paul meant in Philippians 3:10–12. Therefore, trial and tribulation have purpose in making us more Christ-like; and that, my friends, prepares the Bride, not cause Her harm.

Jesus wants to marry a pure Bride. The Church, the Bride of Christ, must enter the Tribulation for Her purification. If She doesn't, She won't be a pure Bride for Her Groom and Lord, Jesus Christ. Right now, She is not pure. There is still worldliness in Her. But He will come for Her when She is prepared and pure—and She will be. It is when She is most pure that the light of Her beauty will shine most brightly. It is Her destiny. It's not a matter of Her forgiveness but character.

The pre-trib rapture view would deny the Bride Her purification, and this would deny the Lord the fulfillment of His mystery, of which He *will not* be denied. For we see, in Revelation during the tribulation period, both, the mystery of iniquity and the mystery of God fulfilled. Since the fulfillment of the mystery of God is directly connected to the seventh and last trumpet as read in Revelation 10:7, and the rapture is connected to and is signaled by the last trumpet blown in Revelation 11:15, then it is evident that the Church, the Bride of Christ, would be present for Her purification. This is a good thing God has planned.

Notice in Jesus's letter to the seven churches, He never addresses, commends nor condemns them about church size and budgets. These don't impress Him. He addresses their character, and their obedience to His will for each. This is what He is after with His Church.

So, when Jesus returns, it isn't to rescue the Christian Church (His Bride) from the world. Why would that be the reason? We must believe He has provided all the Church needs to be overcomers and more than conquerors in *every* situation in the earth (Rom. 8:31–39).

In closing, in Christ's death on the cross, we have been made free from wrath, and we will be delivered from experiencing the wrath that is not for us, Beloved. He loves His Bride and always has Her best interests in mind to present Her as pure. Don't be troubled. He is and will be with us. He promised. Now, we can understand that the rapture will occur when it is time to fulfill God's mysterious purpose, to make ready His Bride (which *is* part of that purpose), and to keep us from the hour of wrath, but not necessarily the tribulation. Keep reading.

TESTING FOR THE JEWS?

Well, the Tribulation is a time of testing for the Jews, not Gentiles . . . you know, 'Jacob's trouble' and all that!

It may be—maybe. Still, this doesn't mean Christians will be exempt from experiencing it. Allow a few examples. Do you remember God's Old Testament command to the Jews, to not harm nor take advantage of foreigners who live among them? In Exodus 22:21, God commanded they not mistreat foreigners who chose to live among them.

Immigrants have always lived among the Israelite people. Beginning with their deliverance from Egyptian slavery, foreign and mixed (Num. 11:4) race peoples came out with them, and continued to live among and 'intermingle' with them (Exodus 12:38, Neh. 13:3). When Babylon captured the Israelites, these foreigners who lived among them were carried away just the same, suffering along with the Israelite people even though the direct discipline was not for them. They weren't filtered out, released and excluded because they were not Israelites.

Presently in cities where we live, how many of us suffer under the curse of crimes by others and by the choices of government officials? We may not cause societies curses but this doesn't mean we are exempt from their effects.

Nothing in the Bible indicates there will be a separation and distinguishing between Jew and Gentiles in the Tribulation. The Bible says the hour of trial is going to come on the entire world to test the inhabitants of the earth (Rev. 3:10). If the Tribulation Period is a time of testing only for Jews, as this is pitched as a reason Christians supposedly wouldn't be on earth, what is the explanation for all the other non-Jew ethnic groups in the world who will be present to experience it, according to the premise?

John Darby, in 1828 England, formed his pre-trib rapture view from what he interpreted as a distinction of Israel and the Church in Ephesians.[4] Sure, there is a distinction between the two groups, but Paul's letter to the Ephesians in chapters 1 through 3 explains the plan in God's beautiful mystery *to unite* Jew and Gentile under His flag in one Body, *not separate* (Eph. 2:11–18; 3:5–6). Where is this passage's language pointing to a pre-trib rapture and the Church's exemption from the Tribulation? Nowhere. He may have wanted this difference to be some kind of reason the Church will escape the trials, but it just isn't substantiated so. Besides, I've never known of or have ever read of God doing one thing with one purpose in mind for only one person or one people group with no further effect to any other(s). He is a multi-function, multi-intention God, always layering purposes for multiple effects and maximum result. *If* the Tribulation is a period of testing for Jews only, this assumption alone is not enough to explain why Christians should not be present during the tribulation period.

CHAPTER FIFTEEN

THE PRE-TRIB RAPTURE TEACHING

In this book's first section, where the rapture occurs in the Book of Revelation is revealed. Since the Bible disagrees with the pre-trib rapture view, we should investigate the origin of this idea. How did this view begin? Did early Christians believe this? What does the Bible really say about the pre-trib rapture stance?

PRE-TRIB HISTORY

One Christian generation propagates another and stands on the shoulders of the former. As stones laid upon others build a temple, their work was laid upon the effort of others before them. Tenets and teachings were passed along, but what was present with them was also the hazard for error and deviation.

It's been speculated a few of the first and second century Early Church fathers like Irenaus, Augustine, Clement and others may have considered the pre-trib rapture view. Maybe some did; maybe some didn't. I've read a couple of articles posting this theory. There's not enough record to substantiate this premise. I think these researchers *read more in between the lines* of a few select quotes by one or two Early Church fathers. However, whatever any Early Church fathers believed makes for no determinate verdict.

We can reason their living closer to the first century church and teachings from the mouth of the first apostles would be most error-free. Let's not forget that almost half of the New Testament apostolic letters continually warned believers to look out for hollow doctrines and errors. They were closer to when and where the truth began, but there were also many distorted teachings spread about infiltrating ancient Christian societies. It's good to know what the second and third century fathers taught and thought, but their words are not inspired-scripture; therefore we cannot take what they said *only* as truth any more than my own words. Even if we cite ten thousand persons who believe this or that—it doesn't count. What they instruct must agree with the biblical record. I'm not discrediting any personally; however, I want to be clear—just because somebody wrote or said something a long time ago doesn't make it true and truth. People of any time period can be off-base on an issue. Take, for example, the apostle Peter. He and Paul had fellowship with Gentile believers. In Mosaic Law, it was forbidden for a Jew to fellowship and dine with a Gentile. When Jewish-Christian church leaders from Jerusalem came to visit to learn about the state of the ministry, Peter feared what the Jerusalem brothers would think of him and withdrew his fellowship from the Gentile brethren. This could have injured the work. So Paul corrected Peter on his error publicly in love. It just goes to show us, even persons who walk close with Jesus can still be wrong and need their thinking corrected.

One Church father examined, who has been quoted to align with the pre-trib rapture view, was Irenaus. His book, *Against Heresies: Book V,* I found to agree with God's Word and nothing of the pre-trib notion.[1,2,3]

Any person's teaching should align with the inspired-scripture. Teaching without biblical agreement show they are non-evidential speculation, some of which stretch scripture. Let's be aware of this.

In 1998, LaHaye published *Rapture Under Attack,* an attempt to firm up this view due to rising and opposing contradictions, hence the book's name. Within it, Grant Jeffery is quoted discovering an old manuscript by Pseudo-Ephrem, (a scroll which may or may not have been written by Ephrem of Nisibis) written between 565 and 627 AD. He purportedly stated the rapture will happen before the Tribulation.[4] This pseudo writer provided no biblical scripture to affirm his comment; therefore Pseudo-Ephrem's statement alone just doesn't make it so. Besides, Ephrem died in 373 AD, 190 to 250 years before this Syriac and Latin pseudepigraphal manuscript was written. How then can this suspect document be offered as proof?

Articles and submissions exist, which position this pre-trib notion as a new doctrine, beginning in America in the mid-18th century. Before this time, no pre-trib rapture teaching is found in America. The pre-trib rapture position was almost only an American theological ideal of Christian living without the threat of suffering and tribulation. The best documentation shows this view began around mid-1700s in the American colonies.[5]

Morgan Edwards is attributed as the first to write and

speak on this idea, expounding upon his end time view in a senior college essay.[6,7] In 1744, Morgan's paper entitled 'Two Academical Exercises on Subjects Bearing Titles; Millennium and Last-Novelties', placed the Antichrist's appearance and self-appointed god position on earth three and a half years before where the two witnesses are killed in Revelation 11. He also symbolized many end-time features, among others, like the celestial signs to not be actual astronomic events but to be figurative of "wars and rumors of wars." [8] My only guess is he couldn't conceive such astronomical events as real. Among other points, he didn't corroborate his thoughts literally with plain scripture, but seemed to read more into them. It's hard to understand how Edwards's essay was received seriously enough to start a new doctrine.

In the nineteenth century, lawyer-preacher John Darby, who was influenced by Morgan's teaching, came along. In 1861, he endorsed a prophetic word by Margaret McDonald, a woman who was part of a sect from England called the "Irvingites", the forerunners of the Catholic Apostolic Church.[9,10] Margaret McDonald and her prophetic word can hardly be enough for a new doctrine. Darby believed her prophetic word to be evidence of a pre-trib rapture. Tim LaHaye used this same prophetic message in his book in effort, I suppose, to add credence to this view.[11] It is interesting that Baptists, who today question whether all the Holy Spirit's gifts are still in play today, didn't seem to have trouble accepting this woman's prophetic gift and word. I have read the prophetic message McDonald received. It contains elements of Christ's return, but there are no phrases perceptibly leaning to a pre-trib rapture concept unless more is assumed. From what we know, *she* never claimed her word articulated a pre-trib rapture.

From 1862 to 1877, Darby formulated and taught his pre-trib perspective, attracting audiences with the suffering-free doctrine.[12] Still, McDonald's prophecy, Morgan's essay, and Darby's messages on the subject are non-evidential. This rapture-tribulation view was further popularized in the book *Jesus Is Coming* written by evangelist William Blackstone in 1878, selling nearly a million copies.[13] C. I. Schofield, another proponent, was influenced by Darby's teaching. He published his own Bible version in 1909 wherein he could easily interject the teaching into its verse notes.[14]

The pre-trib rapture teaching then received a boost in 1957 when Dallas Baptist Theological Seminary professor, Dr. John Walvoord, wrote a book on the matter called, *The Rapture Question.*[15]

I think because some of these early pre-trib authors/preachers were Baptists is reason why latter Baptists readily accepted and preached their tenets on the subject, with inadequate scrutiny.

In 1970, Hal Lindsey's book, *The Late Great Planet Earth*, sold millions of copies and re-popularized talk about the rapture. Its chapter on the rapture is very short, and not categorically clear about its position to the Tribulation. Its main theme is end-times world circumstances, Christ's return, and the Antichrist.

About twenty years later, Tim LaHaye and Jerry Jenkins' Christian fiction series, *Left Behind,* became wildly popular in the 1990s, selling over 60 million copies with many readers asserting belief in the pre-trib rapture view.

The good job of mass marketing is one reason this belief

spread widely. However, popularity and book sales don't prove something is true and factual. Another reason for the popularity is that most Christians have never taken the time to carefully study it for themselves, but simply accepted what they were told. It was a long time before I ever studied it.

In *Rapture Under Attack*, LaHaye quoted Dr. Walvoord stating, 'some people reject the pre-trib rapture position because it is not spelled out in one single passage.'[16] Here, one of the foremost proponents of the perspective, admitted there is no single sentence for a pre-trib rapture event, as agreed Tim LaHaye. They were both right. I agree with them. There isn't. He also said Revelation 4:1–2 by itself would never unlock the mystery of the rapture, but because that event is disclosed in other passages 'one may appropriately identify John's call up to heaven as a rapture event', construing it as the rapture.[17] I agree the passage by itself would never unlock the mystery because it says nothing pertaining to the rapture. I agree the rapture is characterized in other biblical passages, and I acknowledge the incident of John's vision and His being taken up in spirit. However, I disagree that we may appropriately iden- tify this as a rapture event. Why would it be? How can it appropriately be identified as a rapture event? Just saying it does not make it so. LaHaye stated this, but never clarified how. No passages that say anything about the rapture, ever mention Apostle John or anything about him receiving this vision in Revelation 4:1–2. There are no rapture-identifying markers to this. Therefore, these verses cannot appropri- ately identify John's call up to heaven as a rapture event or even to an allusion. In fact, it would be inappropriate to do so. To construe it as such would not be a literal or good interpretation. I have read many pre-trib authors stating a literal interpretation will naturally present a pre-trib view, particularly with Revelation 4:1–2.[18] That's just not so, as we saw in chapter eight. Literal interpretations of Revelation 4:1–2 cannot make agreement with a pre-trib rapture view.

As we saw, a literal interpretation actually proves otherwise. It is a great stretch to even make a figurative interpretation out of Revelation 4:1–2. From the pre-trib authors' books I have read who say they believe in a literal interpretation of the Bible, I haven't found them doing so with this passage. LaHaye said Revelation 4:1–2 cannot be used as a primary rapture teaching.[18] I agree we cannot because it is not a passage about the rapture.

Walvoord was quoted to say there is no verse saying Jesus *wouldn't come* before the Tribulation.[20] Actually, there is. Second Thessalonians 2:1–3 confirms when Jesus would come in relation to the Tribulation . . . *until/unless first* the apostasy occurs and the debut of the Wicked One. *Until,* or *unless first* conveys something follows *after.*

In *Rapture Under Attack,* Second Thessalonians 2:8 was cited to show the cruel one is revealed *after* Christ comes and after the rapture.[21] It doesn't.

Here's the verse. "And then the lawless one will be revealed, whom the Lord Jesus will overthrow with the breath of His mouth and destroy by the splendor of His coming." What words in this verse indicate the rapture? None. What terms in this verse show relation of His coming to the 'lawless one's revealing? None. In the passage context, *And then* relates to the one who restrains quits restraining.

We can't attest to be biblical doctrine what is *not*

written and described in scripture. Still, these author's statements do not substantiate Jesus' return and our rapture before the Tribulation. LaHaye affirmed well his personal pre-trib beliefs, and I appreciate the honesty in admitting when he had no scriptural support for some of them.

During the 2020 pandemic outbreak, *Tipping Point,* a more recent book about Christ's coming and the rapture, was released. The author said Jesus referred to two raptures, one in Luke 17 as the pre-trib rapture and the one in Matthew 24 for saints in the Tribulation Period.[22] Let's look at Luke 17:24, 26–36.

> Jesus said to the disciples, "For as the lightning, that lighteneth out of the one part under heaven, shineth unto the other part under heaven; so shall also the Son of man be in his day . . . And as it was in the days of Noe, so shall it be also in the days of the Son of man. They did eat, they drank, they married wives, they were given in marriage, until the day that Noe entered into the ark, and the flood came, and destroyed them all. Likewise also as it was in the days of Lot; they did eat, they drank, they bought, they sold, they planted, they built; But the same day that Lot went out of Sodom it rained fire and brimstone from heaven, and destroyed them all. Even thus shall it be in the day when the Son of man is revealed. In that day, he which shall be upon the housetop . . . let him not come down to take it away: and he that is in the field, let him likewise not return back . . . I tell you, in that night there shall be two men in one bed; the one shall be taken, and the other shall be left. Two women shall be grinding together; the one shall be taken, and the other

left. Two men shall be in the field; the one shall be taken, and the other left."

In this passage, Jesus said His coming will be quick like lightning, and it would be like it was up to the day Noah entered the ark and Lot left Sodom—people living life, marrying, planting, drinking, buying and selling, unaware of the impending judgment. The author purposes the 'buying and selling' people will conduct as evidence of worldwide economic stability, thus a reason the rapture doesn't occur after the Tribulation starts. He assumes 'buying and selling' is evidence of global economic security, a pre-tribulation condition; and the inability to buy and sell, a condition of the Tribulation Period.[23]

First, this passage says nothing regarding trials, fiscal prosperity or instability, but simply that people continued life's pursuits amidst great immorality and the looming judgment, as in the days of Noah and in Sodom. Just because people will carry on life's activity doesn't mean Luke 17 proves a pre-trib rapture.

There have been many great financial collapses in our world's history and people never ceased buying and selling. If individuals and families couldn't buy and sell as they once did, trade always continued by somebody somewhere. During the national and global economic disaster of the Great Depression, which lasted nearly ten years from 1929 into the late 1930s, people continued to buy and sell, marry, have children, attend school, plant crops, etc., as they could besides other life pursuits. So then, I put forth whether there is prosperity or lack, people will pursue life activities. Once the tribulations begin, there will be instability, but that does not mean economic trade will cease. As long as people have the resources and means, they will continue transacting business.

Second, Jesus' prediction here denotes the rapture will be unexpected, just as when the Great Flood came and when Sodom was destroyed. The disappearance of people will surprise those who remain. No words used here by Jesus precede the rapture to the Tribulation, so I don't understand how this view is reached.

Third, what we can say Jesus showed here is an on-the-ground level experience for people in the rapture; whereas in Matthew 24:30–31, He depicted a higher from-the-air view of the rapture. These aren't two different raptures, but two different viewpoints of it.

In every gospel passage, Jesus spoke of the rapture singularly, not plurally: as did Paul. I note Jesus and Paul place the rapture event with His coming, not separate from the other. His Coming is one monumental event composed of other events, one of which is the rapture.

I want to say I have never been shown verses, by any person alleging the pre-trib rapture, which cooperates congruently with scripture. I have asked fellow ministers over the last thirty-plus years to provide any evidence because I wanted to think it true, too. None have provided any that positively posts the rapture before the Tribulation —just conjecture.

There are a few 'pre-trib rapture' social media sites. Whenever I ask members to share verses that plainly indicate a pre-trib rapture, they can't. No book I have read by any pre-trib author confirms it. Many believe it to be true, but they can't validate it harmoniously with the Bible's text, but only by the theory of some other author, preacher, or commentator.

THE PRE-TRIB RAPTURE VIEW IN THE NEW TESTAMENT

Earlier in this chapter, the pre-trib rapture view was referenced to be a new doctrine since only the late 18ᵗʰ century in America. That is true, and I thought it was relatively new, too, from writings and documents I've read. Some scholars have tried to solidify this rapture position by associating a few of the early Church fathers into the pre-trib rapture camp, not with adequate success. However, after a fresh insight, I now think this view did actually begin back in Paul's day. Let's more closely examine at a clue from Paul's letter.

Okay, by now we know the rapture happens in Revelation 14:14-16 and is not pre-trib. Why go further?

Yes, but I want to show additionally what the apostle Paul said about this pre-trib rapture view. Here's the passage I found interesting and important.

> Concerning the coming of our Lord Jesus Christ and our being gathered to him, we ask you, brothers and sisters, not to become easily unsettled or alarmed by the teaching allegedly from us—whether by a prophecy or by word of mouth or by letter—asserting that the day of the Lord has already come. Don't let anyone deceive you in any way, for that day will not come *until* the rebellion occurs and the man of lawlessness is revealed . . . (2 Thess. 2:1–3 [NIV] Emphases added)

So, from Second Thessalonians 2:1–3, what do we know? First, notice Paul placed Jesus's coming and "our gathering together to Him" in verse one to the same "day of the Lord" at the end of verse two—two pieces connected under the one and same, broad banner, "the day of the Lord." Next, Paul drew the Thessalonians believers' attention to reject a rumor or teaching that Jesus returned, the rapture had taken place and they missed it. How do we know? Paul addressed, "Now concerning the coming of our Lord Jesus Christ and our being gathered together to him . . . we ask you brothers not to be quickly shaken in your mind or alarmed, . . . to the effect that the day of the Lord has come" (2 Thess. 2:1–2). The persons who spread this obviously knew enough teaching about Christ's return and the rapture to get it wrong. With the sufferings and persecutions towards believers of that day, perhaps these who spread the teaching believed Jesus came and they missed Him, or it was just a lie meant to deceive. Either way, Paul thought the matter serious enough to address it. Apparently, this hoax could deceive believers, distressing them. He admonished believers not to be duped by whatever form it came to them (2 Thess. 2:3a). The KJV says "to be not shaken, or be troubled . . . nor by letter *as* from us . . ." (2 Thess. 2:2). He cautioned them, *don't even believe it came from me* (I paraphrase). Let's deduce further.

Paul explained how events would transpire. "Let no one deceive you in any way. For *that day* will not come, unless the rebellion comes *first* and the man of lawlessness is revealed" (2 Thess. 2:3 ESV, Emphasis added). So then, what would this deception have led Thessalonian Christians to believe? This deception would have led them to believe Jesus had come and gathered together believers to Himself *before* the great defiance (falling away) occurred and the antichrist is exposed—pretty clear, huh? I've skimmed over it many times before missing this finer point.

How can what he said be misunderstood now? Paul said these two things will occur first: the rebellion and the lawless one revealed; then these two things will happen: Christ's coming and our being gathered together to Him. Evidently, this teaching that asserted Christ had returned and gathered together His people *before* these two events (the rebellion and revealing of the son of perdition) took place was a deception, according to the apostle Paul.

Hmm.

These are Holy Spirit-inspired words to Paul. How can anyone argue this? This is an instance when we may wrestle with scriptural truth contrasted against what we thought to be true.

The Enemy will twist anything of and from God that he can. He will convince people some food or drink is wrong and a sin when God said its all good and clean when received with thanksgiving. He will tempt you to sin, then turn around and condemn you for doing what he tempted you to do. And he will contort prophecies that were meant to prevent our alarm so that when they don't happen as he falsely led us to believe, we would be alarmed and rattled. Paul said I'm telling you these two things will occur first so you *won't* be shaken.

Here's the lie, again: Jesus came and gathered believers before the rebellion occurred and the lawless man was revealed.

Which tribulation-rapture view that you know today matches this?

Think for a minute.

Let me rephrase the question. Which view today says Jesus will come and gather His people *before* the rebellion occurs and the man of lawlessness (Antichrist) be revealed?

The pre-trib rapture view.

No, the Bible doesn't use the phrase *pre-trib rapture view,* but the key pieces of it fit the fraud Paul described. What did Paul call this teaching? It's in verse three. A deception. Since he told those believers *don't be deceived,* then this teaching must be a deception. What then should this same teaching today be called?

We can also reason, since this fallacy circulated during Paul's day, it likely continued to circulate, could have been picked up by unwary believers, and passed along years later to and by any of the second century Church fathers forward to this day. This would explain why one or two of them *might* have believed in a pre-trib rapture view. It must be plausible, *if* any did, because it was possible.

We must elevate God's Word and proper interpretation over men's words that are not inspired by the Holy Spirit. Jesus chided the Pharisees because they equalized men's words and traditions with God's commands. There are many well-known preachers I respect and feel a high regard for, whose books I've read, sermons I've heard and whom I've met in-person; some, whom have passed on to heaven. However, I can't elevate their words over Holy Scripture no matter how much I like them, and from heaven's view—I think they'd want it that way. Let's make sure we're not holding onto a teaching by anyone, appealing to our ease, comfort, and human sympathy, but conflicts with the Bible. We must adhere to Jesus and Paul's testimonies over any other commentary.

Not only does Revelation 14:14–16 totally disprove this view by itself, but this Second Thessalonian passage is damning to the pre-trib rapture view—not to people who believe it or taught it, but to the teaching itself which Paul specified is a deception. We need to know then, when world events intensify and Jesus hasn't come yet to rapture us before the rebellion and the Antichrist uncovers, we should not believe a lie that Jesus came and we've been left. To repeat Paul, don't be alarmed or unsettled. It will be the same lie told during Paul's day.

DISSONANCE AND DISBELIEF

It can be hard to accept that something we've taught and believed for such a long time has never been correct. As I composed this chapter, the Lord put the word *dissonance* in my mind. I figured it had to be germane to what people believe about this so I googled it.

There are a couple of meanings. Musically, it means there is a disagreement or clashing of musical intervals or chords: a disharmony in composition. It also means an inconsistency or disagreement in beliefs.

Cognitive dissonance is what people experience when their long-held belief, value or moré is presented with new or newly understood evidence to the contrary. It is the difficulty in accepting new evidence. One may feel that it is so important to protect their long-held stance that they will rationalize away, ignore or even deny the newly understood evidence. When this happens, dissonance becomes disbelief. For example, the Pharisees couldn't bring themselves to accept Jesus' teaching because it was disharmonious and conflicted with their long-held pharisaical beliefs. They wouldn't entertain the thought that maybe what they believed was wrong. For any of us who believed the pre-trib rapture view, we may feel the disagreement and the disharmony between what we have believed and what is now realized in Revelation. We're human; we believed what we were told. But how can we now deny what the Bible reveals about the rapture's position? Whenever biblical evidence clashes with what we have believed, we should believe the biblical evidence. His Word continually challenges my thinking, as it should. I am so glad it does because otherwise I would be stuck in old, irrelevant and unfruitful thinking. No doubt it will still be defended since many believed it and some still teach it. My hope is like Apostle Paul's, that none would become alarmed or unsettled by how future events will play out.

Concluding, what we did previously throughout this book is look in Revelation for where the markers Jesus and Paul gave us would occur—impartially wherever they might be. We saw the rapture described in Revelation 14: 14–16 fits just as Jesus described it in the gospel accounts. And coupled with Paul's rapture description and clues, everything matches and interlocks in Revelation; leading us to this eventual conclusion—the rapture does not occur before the Tribulation. More believers are realizing the pre-tribulation rapture inconsistencies. This notion has been a deception and, now is a casualty of truth.

There is more for us to hope. Before I get to that, I want to say something next about the last generation.

PART THREE

CHAPTER SIXTEEN

A GENERATION

Now that we found where the rapture lies in Revelation, the thought of going through any part of The Adversity may cause uneasy feelings. Paul wanted believers to know the order of events before Christ comes so they would *not* be distressed. He taught believers would escape the hour of wrath, not the Tribulation. The pre-trib view has misled a generation to believe they will avoid the misery altogether. One person said to me, "How then is going through the Tribulation comforting?" I replied, "It's not. But God's promises to comfort us, to be our help, and our provision, are." Here's the thing—a generation has to enter and experience the Tribulation. Somebody must. It's prophesied.

Generations of God's people throughout history underwent serious and frightening times. Consider the ten generations of Israelites who endured four hundred years of Egyptian enslavement. Reflect on the Israelite generation who lived forty years in the Wilderness. There had to be a generation. Take into account the Israelite generations who survived the Midian and Assyrian occupations, and the Babylonian Captivity.

Imagine what Israel was like in Jesus' generation while under Roman control and occupation. Both Roman and Jewish governments were corrupt, and justice was rare. Taxation was high. Roman soldiers could take whatever they wanted from the Jews. Women, widows, and fatherless children were very vulnerable and exploited. It has been estimated up to half of the population was enslaved in the known world. Anybody thought to be dissident to government could be mocked, beaten, imprisoned, or crucified. Jewish religious leaders persecuted and ran out-of-town anyone who opposed pharisaical Judaism. Moreover, the modern utilities and conveniences which make life much easier today didn't exist then. It was a very inhospitable world compared to now. And Christianity was birthed in just such a time, full of hardship.

The Early Church Christians suffered for Christ. More generations followed who lived through several hundred years of inhumane Roman persecutions. Generations of ethnic groups around the world have suffered horribly because of their color, belief, or their ethnicity. The point is there is always a generation enduring hardship in the world somewhere. And so on earth, there must be a generation surviving the Tribulation Period.

People will be in different life stages when it occurs. Some elderly people's retirement will be shortened. They may be fifty-year-olds whose plans were to retire but then won't be able, or adults who never see grandchildren born, and parents who never see their child graduate high school or attend a prom; or a teenager who doesn't get to enjoy college, marriage, or childbirth. Some children will never experience driving a car because the tribulation effects will cut into normal life events. Though all this will be, we do not stop living life's adventures, but continue. Jesus said before He comes, it would be as it was up to the day of the Great Flood: people were eating, drinking and marrying. Some people won't experience things past generations did.

But for the last generation, we will see things no previous generation ever did. We will see huge supernatural works—and many of them. Global prophecies will fulfill before our very eyes. If you ever asked the Lord to show you His glory and power, this will be the time to see it. Heavenly phenomena and wondrous miracles on earth! God is pouring out His Spirit on the earth, even now, just as He said. For whenever in history, God poured out His Spirit, great revivals broke out with signs and miracles. We will see soon a Great Revival rise and spread over the earth, full of spectacular miracles of all kinds performed by believers across denomination lines. At no other time will we see more miraculous phenomena take place around the world on local, global and cosmic scales. Aside from Christ's crucifixion and resurrection, this will be the greatest show on earth and in the heavens—the grandest display of God's power ever, and—He saved it for last! Just as the water He turned into wine was the best and served last, He will pour out the best on His people when it seems there's no hope and nothing left. We will see His mysterious plan of the ages materialize on earth, climaxing in the rapture. Ephesians 1: 10 says God's agenda 'to gather together in one all things in Christ, both which are in heaven, and which are on earth; even in Him:' will be fulfilled. What saints and prophets of old only imagined, we will realize. We will see the Lord's return with our very eyes. It will be amazing to watch and glorious to encounter. As He has been faithful throughout all history, He will be still. He will never let His people down. He promised.

CHAPTER SEVENTEEN

DOES IT REALLY MATTER?

I'm sure you have heard it said by many people *It doesn't matter when the rapture takes place. I'm not worrying about it. It'll happen when it happens.*

I don't want any to worry about it, but I want to be prepared. Here's my question: If it's not important when, then why did God inspire it to be written about and included in scriptural canon? If God didn't want it to be known with the sequential events, why give the details? If it doesn't matter to you when it happens, do you accept it will occur in Revelation 14?

People rejected the Old Testament prophets' messages. Why would God give them a prophetic word foretelling good and bad news? So they would know it, repent or prepare. Jesus could have simply said, *Hey yeah, I'm returning. Just know it'll happen in the last days.* Is that all He said? No, He was more specific than that, given the details we've read. He provided us them so we wouldn't be deceived by bogus doctrines, spurious teachers, or counterfeit Christs. He warned us, *beware.*

I believe we have moved into a new era since *Covid-19* came on the scene. It's an accelerating ingredient in preparing the way for future events to unfold like greater government control, which will be a part of the antichrist government. I have said for ten plus years that censorship against whatever is Christian is coming to social media and culture. Now here it is, and watch it increase. Very soon, sharing the gospel will be hate speech. Dark forces will have their heyday in shaming whoever and whatever is Christlike. It will be said a move to a cashless society is necessary for financial integrity and security in the world. Financial experts expect its implementation five years from Fall 2020. This will be a factor in introducing the 'mark of the beast'. It will be said for the sake of the planet's survival all people need to do this and that, but these will be means to advance the antichrist's agenda for control.

The working of evil powers in people will become open and bold, but so will the boldness and working of the Holy Spirit in Christians. I believe we are going to see a charismatic revival, as has been every major renewal in the world. It will come upon the land, spreading out across the country and the globe. Supernatural power of the Holy Spirit will manifest through believers. It is now—and it is increasing! Since it will happen in my lifetime, I don't want to miss it.

Second reason, knowing when He will rapture us should give us great hope, whenever it occurs. After all, seeing and being with Him is what saints have been waiting for, right? It's what He has been awaiting. To know we will escape the worst and that He will take us out of this world from all its negativity, disease, trauma, and offense is a great comfort. The Book of Revelation is a message of warning to the unbelieving and a message of hope to the saved. Knowing tribulations are coming doesn't bring consolation, but knowing the promise that God will be our Comfort, is.

The third reason the Lord wants us to know what to look for is to impress urgency. Urgency is a great motivator. Jesus used urgency in His preaching. Often, He urged people to act for the hope of gain in the kingdom or the fear of loss. Particularly, he wanted to unseat the 'unsaved' so they will come to a saving faith in Him. It is for *them* to realize the importance of the saving gospel message and for believers to feel the urgency to thread their conversations with the good news and His return.

I have a fifteen-second, elevator speech memorized, ready to share when time with someone is limited. If you don't have one, create one or use this one. It goes like this, *Hey, I've got some good news for you. God's kingdom has come. Jesus Christ died on the cross for your sins and rose from the dead so you can be saved and receive eternal life. His return is near and His forgiveness is available to anyone who asks.* That's it— the gospel in short, to the point: urgent.

With three years to accomplish what He needed, Jesus had to focus, be intent and urgent. He repeated the Kingdom was near, at hand, and has come. He told many urgent parables to motivate people to act, watch, and be ready. Knowing time limits helps us prioritize. That's something I hope this does for readers.

Look at the people around you as you go through your day, where you work, when you shop or vacation. Will they be one of those fully ripe grapes? They need a believer to share with them the saving gospel now before it's too late for them. Then your feet will be called beautiful (Isa. 52:7).

Fourth point: be prepared. Who likes to be unprepared? No one really does. If we don't prepare, we probably want someone else to prepare for us. We plan for many life contingencies and try to manage risks. People living in coastal areas will plan for hurricanes. We prepare by having for ourselves now a supply of food. We save money to prepare for unforeseen accidents and expenses, and retirement. We plan for our children and for our protection. And so, we ought to prepare for this.

In one pre-trib book, an author said the Bible doesn't instruct us to prepare for this. Not true. In the Parable of the Ten Virgins, they were instructed to be ready, rehearsed and prepared for the bridegroom's coming. Some virgins planned, having oil and their wicks trimmed: some did not and they missed the bridegroom. You will find the word 'prepare' and its verb forms well over one hundred times in the Bible. Jesus is giving us a heads up to prepare. But prepare how? We each may have different material resources but there are ways we all can prepare. It'll take some thought because we need to adjust our mindset: leave behind an incorrect view we held for so long and now wrap our minds around this biblical one. How can we prepare? Here are some ways, in brief.

BE WATCHFUL

Matthew 24:37–45 is a passage about preparing by being watchful.

> But as the days of Noe were, so shall also the coming of the Son of man be. For as in the days that were before the flood they were eating and drinking, marrying and giving

in marriage, until the day that Noe entered into the ark, And knew not until the flood came, and took them all away; so shall also the coming of the Son of man be . . .Watch therefore: for ye know not what hour your Lord doth come. Therefore keep watch, because you do not know on what day your Lord will come. But understand this: If the owner of the house had known at what time of night the thief was coming, he would have kept watch and would not have let his house be broken into. *So you also must be ready*, because the Son of Man will come at an hour when you do not expect him." (Emphasis mine)

In Mark 13:32–37 Jesus said,

Take ye heed, watch and pray: for ye know not when the time is. For the Son of Man is as a man taking a far journey, who left his house, and gave authority to his servants, and to every man his work, and commanded the porter to watch. Watch ye therefore: for ye know not when the master of the house cometh, at even, or at midnight, or at the cockcrowing, or in the morning: Lest coming suddenly he find you sleeping. And what I say unto you I say unto all, Watch.

We have His admonition to watch for His return. Watching is preparation. It is expectancy. It's a mindset. It is attending—looking with expectant faith for the reality that He will come just as He said. Let us refresh our anticipation, believing we are on the cusp of His return. If we watch, then our minds will expect. A righteous focus towards others and the awareness of His imminence will develop, for certainly His return is ever increasingly closer.

BE COMMUNAL

I know this—believers will need each other until that blessed day comes. We will return to a church life as seen in the Book of Acts. The Church will move from denominational/building-centered congregations to organic, decentralized, ecumenical fellowships focused on our Master, Jesus Christ. Any who are family by the blood of Jesus should meet often to encourage one another and do life together in the Word and worship. Fellowship and Christian community will be vital to enduring, pooling resources, and providing emotional and spiritual support, just as the Church did years ago. Sharing material resources will be practical, but ultimately, we will trust God's provision. Spiritual giftedness will flower. More home churches will form out of the supernatural gravity of believers to coalesce wherever they can. They will be intimate, personal, beautiful, and powerful. We will maneuver like wise serpents and harmless doves dealing with those 'outside' the Body, as 'underground' churches have learned to exist in inhospitable cultures around the world. A life participating in an authentic church fosters abiding in Him. If you don't mutually take part in a local church body, find one you can. Though digital technology has advanced the outward reach of the local church (it is better than not attending in-person), nothing beats the presence and touch of physical fellowship. He will remain as much God as He ever was and we will know Him intimately.

We need never forget He highly favors us—the apple of His eye, His Beloved that He looks upon with intense desire. He will always be with us. He promised.

BE PATIENT AND HAVE FAITH

As temperatures rise against anything Christian, Jesus said settle within. When facing accusers in a courtroom, governmental office, or jail, He said don't prepare what you will say. In such case, the preparation is don't prepare. You won't need to plan what to say. He will give you supernaturally by the Holy Spirit what to reply to any accusation. "But make up your mind not to worry beforehand how you will defend yourselves. For I will give you words and wisdom that none of your adversaries will be able to resist or contradict" (Luke 21:14 NIV).

We especially need patience. Apostle Paul wrote that the rebellion against all things godly and pertaining to God would increase. Patience holds and settles oneself. We need to cultivate this in our heart and soul now. Without patience, we're just beat down. Persevering means we hope in something that hasn't manifested yet. We can outlast difficulty when we know relief will come, a solution on the horizon, our deliverance. Jesus said in Luke 21:19, "In your patience possess your souls." It's when we are impatient, we become unsettled. Jesus said patience would be important. In Revelation, Apostle John was told such times would call for patient endurance, strong faith, and staying faithful to Jesus. Patience and peace are cousins. They are related. They walk together. We cannot surrender to the pressure from society to turn away our faith. We can overcome. He promised.

> But we have this treasure in earthen vessels, that the excellency of the power may be of God, and not of us. We are troubled on every side, yet not distressed; we are

perplexed, but not in despair; Persecuted, but not forsaken; cast down, but not destroyed; Always bearing about in the body the dying of the Lord Jesus, that the life also of Jesus might be made manifest in our body.' (2 Cor. 4:7–10)

Apostle John said,

. . . for everyone born of God overcomes the world. This is the victory that has overcome the world, even our faith. Who is it that overcomes the world? Only the one who believes that Jesus is the Son of God.' (1 John 5:4–5),

Also, "This calls for patient endurance and faithfulness on the part of God's people" (Rev. 13:10). Mark 13:13 says, "And ye shall be hated of all men for my name's sake: but he that shall endure unto the end, the same shall be saved" "This calls for patient endurance on the part of the people of God who keep his commands and remain faithful to Jesus" (Rev. 14:12).

BE FOCUSED

Fixing the eyes of our heart is key. Hiking is one of my pleasures. I enjoy being outside on a nature trail, pressing forward on a climb. I've learned on long hikes it is necessary to fix my eyes on an immovable point like a hill or peak in the distance. It helps gauge my movement and position. It's a stationary marker for when I have a long trek. By it, I know my proximity to my destination. I can tell I'm getting closer and that encourages me. Christ must be our focus, not circumstances and any changes that will take place. In what will be the most chaotic time, He will make sense out of it for us. If we focus our eyes and mind on the chaos, we won't be able to see what God is doing around us. We must see that He is bigger than any circumstance. He is the immovable point and destination we look for. When we see Him, we will reach Him. Know that His eyes are set on you. Nothing can distract His loving gaze. And everyone the Father has given Him, He will not lose. He promised.

Hebrews 12:2–4 states,

> . . . fixing our eyes on Jesus, the pioneer and perfecter of faith. For the joy set before him he endured the cross, scorning its shame, and sat down at the right hand of the throne of God. Consider him who endured such opposition from sinners, so that you will not grow weary and lose heart. In your struggle against sin, you have not yet resisted to the point of shedding your blood.

BE JOYFUL

Did you notice joy in the verse out of Hebrews? Joy is vital for facing, going through, and coming out the other side of difficulties. Psychologists say joy and returning to joy helps endure and survive trauma. Ever notice on old bridges, just before your vehicle rolls onto a bridge, there is a sign stating the bridge's weight capacity? It lets a driver know if their vehicle and the weight it carries are more than the bridge can bear. That's what joy is. Joy is capacity. It provides the capacity to sustain heaviness and hardship. The more joy you have, and the ability to return to joy, helps you bear the heavy loads of life and trial. People, who survive even thrive in the difficulties of life, have joy and an ability to return to joy in or after a trial. The less joy one has, the more easily a trial can overtake one with negativity and despair.

Jesus had such tremendous joy. It enabled Him to see past the horrible torture of the cross set before Him, seeing to the other side what awaited us through His death on the cross. That gave Him joy; a joy that outweighed the trauma He knew He would suffer. We will need joy to do the same.

Amid the turbulent New Testament societies, the disciples spoke of the wondrous things of God. It is important we believe and orally proclaim that God is good. That profession is powerful. The Bible says the Joy of the Lord will be our strength. Ask for joy. Choose joy. Learn to cultivate it now. Make Him the source of your joy. It is His joy that is our strength. He promised.

BE PRAYERFUL

"The end of all things is near. Therefore be alert and of sober mind so that you may pray. Above all, love each other deeply, because love covers over a multitude of sins" (1 Peter 4:7–8). Why? So, you may pray. As pressures intensify, pray. Spiritual dullness and an inattentive mind hinder prayer.

Prayer prepares us. In the Garden of Gethsemane, that hour of His grief, He urged the disciples to pray with Him. Jesus obviously wanted them to grasp the gravity of His return in telling them to watch and pray.

What a wonderful thing it is when our attentions fully look to Him. More than any other time, people of all ages and nations will look to Him with anticipation, desiring His speedy return.

All things, whatever we may trust in, will become uncertain, or be taken away: bank accounts, retirement accounts, insurance or persons. They already are, we just don't see them that way. All things will fall short and He will be proved as the one and only thing, the one and only Person we can trust to provide. It's not enough to simply think it in theory. He wants us to factually know it and be fully persuaded in His promises. He will prove how ultimately faithful He is to His people. He will protect. He will guide. He will be shown most true, most majestic, most powerful, the most beautiful. That's what the last days and Revelation are about—the revealing—the unveiling of Jesus the Christ, our Lord and Saviour displayed in all His glory and majesty. We will see Him as He really is, and it will change us forever—He promised!

CHAPTER EIGHTEEN
A WORD FROM PETER

Apostle Peter left a message for generations about the Lord's return in his letter, Second Peter 3 (I paraphrase part). He said regarding Jesus' promise to return, scoffers will say, *Oh yeah, where is He? It's been a long time and he still hasn't come.* Peter said don't be impatient and don't let what they say dissuade your faith.

"One day with the Lord is a thousand years and a thousand years is as one day." What does that mean? It means God is patient. What seems like a long time for us is really short to Him. He can step outside time and step back in at will, and peer across ages where a thousand years seems like only one day. I believe each six creation-day represented a thousand-year period on earth foretelling He will return at the end of 6000 years from creation (which is very close), and thereafter begin the millennial reign of peace, illustrated by the seventh day of rest.

Why is He delaying His arrival? He's waiting for as many as will to repent. His heart towards people is merciful kindness right now; but as we've learned, one day He'll put that aside and the door of opportunity will close. He will come unexpectedly like a thief does at night.

Lord, help us pay attention to our dull expectation.

Wake up, Church! Wake up!

Remember, the time is coming when He will remake this heaven and earth, so don't hold tightly to earthly things. Live holy lives as you know the day is approaching. Make every effort to be spotless and blameless. *Now, Beloved,* says Peter (I paraphrase), *since I have forewarned you. Be on your guard so that no one may cast a net at your feet, carry you off in the trap of the lawless, that temptation to compromise your faithfulness to the Lord, and fall from your secure position. Be sensitive to the continuous wearing away, the erosion of God's truth in your society. Do not be fooled. Grow in the abundant, beautiful favor Jesus has towards you. Seek experiences with our Saviour, Jesus Christ Himself.*

CHAPTER NINETEEN

NO FEAR IN TRIBULATION

God's love is the greatest force in the Universe. This summer, I had an urge to get away with the Lord. My eldest son and I arranged a trip to visit my eldest sister and her husband in Colorado in 2021, to hike, raft and enjoy the natural beauty of the Sangre de Cristo Mountains. Days before our departure, his work details fell through and he couldn't go with me. I went anyway. Coincidentally, my sister and her husband were called out of town due to a friend's death. I knew this was my opportunity to retreat alone with the Lord.

After I arrived, and as soon as I unpacked my gear, in a matter of minutes, the Lord immediately healed a longtime grief I carried. I had my personal spiritual plan to focus on with Him, but this was unexpected. How often do we seek the Lord about one thing, and then discover He wants to talk about something else? That's when you throw your *agenda out the winda'*. Because He knew every detail of my life, He knew what I needed first. He's good like that. I sensed Him say, *I want to do this first. Trust me.* He was right, as usual. The healing He did in those minutes is another matter. Here's the thing, in that same moment He gave me a glimpse of how great His love is. I thought I knew already how great it is. You know, just when you think you know the Lord and His character well, He surprises you with a revelation of more. For me, it was just one, maybe a two second glimpse. It's hard to quantify. How do you comprehend something so boundless and powerful?

I've heard people refer to the Holy Spirit as a force. He is a Person and He is powerful. I wouldn't say He is a force. What God let me perceive about His love in that moment was enough to know this—His love is the most powerful force in the Universe. It's stronger than all the gravitational forces of every planet, star and black hole. It is the most huge, most incredible supernatural power ever. This love is more than sufficient to quell all the grief and sorrow of every tragedy, in every abusive moment, of every torture suffered, from every sin received from and committed upon every person who ever lived, and surpass it all in peace and love and joy and healing and laughter, with loads left over. Jesus possessed this love within Him on the cross. He embodied it. It's more powerful than all the hate with its effects and the evil the Enemy will dish out, and to whatever amount of measure—if it could be measured, the love God will act with for us is immeasurably more. It's unquenchable, inextinguishable! That's why the cross of Jesus conquers all, and the Enemy hates it. It's more powerful than anything he has. So when Jesus told the disciples, "In this world you will have tribulation, but be of good cheer; I have overcome the world", He confidently knew it by experience. What this means is He's already factored in everything He knows about the future in all detail and He has accommodated for it, for us and in Himself. Since He is in us and we are in Him, we can overcome. It's already been decided and has been completely accomplished in the future and there's no changing it. This is what Paul knew when he wrote in Romans,

> Who will separate us from the love of Christ? Will tribulation, or distress, or persecution, or famine, or nakedness, or peril, or sword? As it is written, For your sake we are killed all the day long; we are accounted as sheep for the slaughter. No, in all these things we are more than conquerors through him that loved us. For I am persuaded, that neither death, nor life, nor angels, nor principalities, nor powers, nor things present, nor things to come, Nor height, nor depth, nor any other creature, shall be able to separate us from the love of God, which is in Christ Jesus our Lord. (Rom. 8:35–39)

God's love in action towards us and in us can be more powerful than all the trouble of the Tribulation. The Enemy would be pleased if he can make us fear the future. Beloved, we need not fret future days. 1 John 4 says mature love casts out all fear.

Learning to abide in His love will be paramount. His love will conquer all; so then His love in us can prevail over all. We must learn to cultivate our ability to abide in His presence and love. Abiding is the practiced delight of spending time with the Lord. It can involve making peaceful physical surroundings for quietness to hear Him. Moreover, it is learning to make the mind and heart within calm for the inner retreat of His presence so that no matter where we are geographically and whoever is around us, we can reside in the Refuge He is within us. This is what the Old Testament psalm meant by 'the Lord is my refuge and my fortress'. Since the cross, He now can abide within us. So since He is within, we can have Him as this inner Refuge and Fortress. It is more than a quiet time. It is learning to dwell in this secret spiritual place within us that is Him (see Ps. 91). You know you are there when the unseen reality of His Person and promises feels just as real as the material things around you. The more we practice His presence, the greater the inner Refuge and Fortress of Him grows within us, and this is how we can be "more than conquerors." This solidifies our faith to overcome the world, as He did with the Father. This is the abiding Jesus spoke of in John 15. Just days before His arrest, He shared this critical secret of abiding, which He knew and practiced with the Father. By this, we saints will have the patience and faith Jesus pledged and John was charged in Revelation.

Be comforted by Apostle John's words from First John 3:2, "Dear friends, now we are children of God, and what we will be has not yet been made known. But we know that when Christ appears, we shall be like him, for we shall see him as he is."

Amen! Moreover, this passage is really meant to be recited to encourage one another.

Brothers and sisters, we do not want you to be uninformed about those who sleep in death, so that you do not grieve like the rest of mankind, who have no hope. For we believe that Jesus died and rose again, and so we believe that God will bring with Jesus those who have fallen asleep in him. According to the Lord's word, we tell you that we who are still alive, who are left until the coming of the Lord, will certainly not precede those who have fallen asleep. For the Lord himself will come down from heaven, with a loud command, with the voice of the archangel and with the trumpet call of God, and the dead in Christ will rise first. After that, we who are still alive and are left will be caught up together with them in the clouds to meet the Lord in the air. And so we will be with the Lord forever. Therefore encourage [comfort] one another with these words.' (1 Thess. 4:13–18 [NIV])

A WORD FROM THE LORD

More than other admonitions found in the Bible, God encourages His people to not fear. Prophetically, He said it in the past. For today and for tomorrow, the LORD still says *I am with you; Yeah, I will never leave you. I will uphold you with my righteous right hand, and I will help you. I will not leave you comfortless, but give you the Comforter. I will help you, I will help you, I will help you because—that's what I do. You are Mine and I am yours. I will be with you through the rivers and waters. They will not overtake you. When you walk through the fire, you will not be burned because I am with you—you won't even smell like smoke.*

I am your Fortress. I am your Refuge, The Holy One of God. I alone am your Shield and your Defense—Me, and I am coming for you. During this time and as these days unfold, the LORD says, *do not fear, I'll be with you. Do not anxiously look about you, for I am your God. I will help you. Look to Me. Look . . . to . . . Me, My beautiful ones. You are mine, and I have called you by name. Your names are written on the palms of My hands. How could I forget you?*

I know the inner struggle you feel so well. I know your

concern. This calls for patience and faith in Me and My promises.

In this time, I will show just how real and strong My promises are. Learn them. Live in them. I want to be glorified. Beloved, I have been looking forward to this day for so long. I'm so excited for it. Trust Me to keep you. Trust Me. I want you to know I love you. I AM here with you. I will help you: I will hold your hand, your right hand. My righteous ones will not be forsaken nor their seed begging for bread.

Do not fear the Darkness. My Light is more powerful. I have overcome them. They can do nothing unless I permit it. Little do they know that what they do will be used by Me to work My will and upgrade your likeness to Mine. They can't stop Me from even using them. This is how I work. Understand that in every trial, there will be an upgrade available, and in every difficulty there is a blessing for you. Look for it. With each one and before each one, there is a promise I have provided by which you can unlock and claim them. For then you will see joy on the other side and endure with faith.

Beloved, know My coronation is set. Know it is near. My arrival will come with such a great execution of power not seen since creation. The day when all will acknowledge Me as KING OF KINGS and LORD OF LORDS is so near. I am so excited about what it means for us, My beloved Bride. Have faith. Hold fast. Cling to My resurrection. I AM coming. I promise. (Isaiah 40:27–31; 41:8–14; 43: 1–5, 13, 18–19; 44:22; 49:16; 51:10–13; 52:9–10; Solomon's Song 8:6–7; John 15:1–11; Romans 8:28; Rev. 13: 10b; Rev. 19; 22:12–21)

God bless you.

APPENDIX

A PRAYER FOR SALVATION

If in reading this you have realized you don't personally know Jesus Christ as your Saviour and Lord, or you are doubting, there's no reason you can't get it settled right here and now. Just pray this prayer aloud with sincerity.

God, I know I am a sinner who needs your forgiveness. I repent and renounce any and every agreement, contract or vow I ever made with Darkness by sinning and believing their lies. I ask you to forgive me of my sins. Cleanse me of my unrighteousness, come into my heart and save me. Seal me with Your Holy Spirit. I believe that You, Jesus, died for my sins and rose again from the dead, and I profess You, Jesus, as God, my Lord, and Saviour. I believe and trust Your promise to save me. I receive You by faith right now. Thank You, Jesus.

You can now be assured you are saved and will be raptured with all the saints; that is who you are now. Believe in His promise to save.

ABOUT THE AUTHOR

Wayne DesLattes is a minister and writer/author living in Louisiana, USA. He has served in ministry since 1990 teaching and pastoring several churches. Wayne has been a published writer in newspaper, and in *Thriving Family*, a Focus On The Family magazine. He has a Bachelor's of Cardio-Pulmonary Science, and studied at New Orleans Baptist Theological Seminary and Louisiana Baptist Theological Seminary, earning a Master's of Theology degree. Wayne also administers healing and deliverance, is founder of Christ's Healing Ministry; and enjoys teaching believer's their identity and inheritance, and exhorting the Church.

Christ's Healing Ministry is dedicated to the healing ministry Jesus Christ started and commissioned to His Body, the Church, for the physical healing, spiritual and inner healing, and deliverance of people.

RESOURCES
AND STAYING CONNECTED

By the publisher email, charismpresspublishing@gmail.com ,
you can:

- be notified when his next books & resources
  release for pre-order;
- be notified of new website, social media,
  newsletter/blog, and video launches;
- schedule a speaking engagement with Wayne.

By Christ's Healing Ministry email, christshealingmin@
gmail.com , you can:

- be notified of new website, social media,
  newsletter/blog & video launches;
- submit a request for a confidential online
  session for healing prayer with the ministry
  team (session availability limited);
- be notified of opportunities to receive healing
  ministry, training & teaching;
- schedule a speaking engagement with Wayne.

REFERENCES

CHAPTER 1

1. George Orwell. *1984*, (New York: Harper Collins, LLC. 1949).
2. Donald W. Thompson, director. *A Thief In The Night*. (Iowa, 1972).
3. Vic Sarin. *Left Behind*. (Canada, 2000).
4. Larry Norman. '*I Wish We'd All Been Ready*', with Fishmarket Combo, (Capitol Records, 1969).

CHAPTER 3

1. "The History of the Rapture"." Biblicaleschatology.org. Last modified December 04, 2008. https://biblicaleschatology. org/2008/12/04/the-history-of-the-rapture/
2. 'nouning'. CollinsDictionary.com. Last modified

August 26, 2020. https://www.collinsdictionary.
com/us/submission/22688/nouning

3. "Turning Nouns Into Verbs". Online Writing
   Training. https://onlinewritingtraining.com.au/
   turning-verbs-into-nouns-nominalisation/

CHAPTER 6

1. James Strong . *Strong's Exhaustive Concordance of
   the Bible*. Iowa Falls: Riverside Book and Bible
   House, 1951.

CHAPTER 8

1. Tim LaHaye. *Rapture Under Attack.* (Sisters:
   Multnomah Publishers, Inc., 1998.) 212.
2. Robert Zemekis. *Back to the Future II.* (United
   States, 1989.)
3. Ibid., 32, 180, 204–210, 212.

CHAPTER 9

1. "What Is the Feast of Trumpets". October 6,
   2020. https://www.biblestudytools.com/bible-
   study/topical-studies/what-is-the-feast-of-
   trumpets.html
2. "Rosh HaShananh — The Feast of Trumpets".
   Accessed December 13, 2021. https://
   promisestoisrael.org/jewish-culture-2/jewish-

holidays/rosh-hashanah-the-feast-of-trumpets/

CHAPTER 10

1. James Strong. *Strong's Exhaustive Concordance of the Bible.* (Iowa Falls: Riverside Book and Bible House, 1951). 380, 32.
2. Lana and Lilly Wachowski. *The Matrix.* (United States and Australia, 1999).

CHAPTER 11

1. George Ricker Berry. *The Interlinear Greek-English New Testament With Lexicon and Synonyms.* (Grand Rapids: Zondervan Publishing House, 1980.) 537.

CHAPTER 12

1. Charles Dickens. *A Tale of Two Cities,* edited by Richard Maxwell. (London: Penguin Classics. 2003).

CHAPTER 14

1. William Collins Sons & Co., LTD. *Collins English Dictionary – Complete & Unabridged 2012 Digital Edition,* :1979, 1986 (New York: Harper Collins Publishing, 2012).

2. Tim LaHaye. *Rapture Under Attack.* 72–73.
3. Ibid., 70–73.
4. Ibid., 162.

CHAPTER 15

1. Irenaus. *Against Heresies, Book V, Chapters 19–31.* https://media-cloud.sermonaudio.com/text/6261891307.pdf.

2. _____. *Ante-Nicene Fathers, Vol. 1.* Translated by Alexander Roberts and William Rambaut, et.al (Buffalo: Christian Literature Publishing Co., 1885). https://www.newadvent.org/fathers/0103519.htm

3. Matt Slick. "Irenaus Against Heresies, Book 5, Chapters 19–31." Carm.org. (July 2010). Early Church Fathers. https://carm.org/irenaus-against-heresies-book-5-chapters-19-31-virgin/

4. Tim LaHaye. *Rapture Under Attack.* (Sisters: Multnomah Publishers, Inc., 1998.) 44.

5. Ibid., 137–170.

6. Ibid., 43.

7. E.R Sandeen. *The Roots of Fundamentalism 1800-1930*, (Chicago: Univ. of Chicago Press, 1970).

8. The Pre-Trib Research Center. "Two Academical Exercises on Subjects Bearing the Following Titles, Millennium and Last Novelties". 17–28. https://www.pre-trib.org/articles/rev-morgan-edwards/message/two-academical-exercises-on-subjects-bearing-the-following-titles-millennium-last-novelties/read

9. Tim LaHaye. *Rapture Under Attack*. (Sisters: Multnomah Publishers, Inc., 1998.) 129–164.

10. Ibid., 129–145.

11. Ibid., 235–238.

12. Ibid., 139–146, 159–160.

13. William Blackstone. *Jesus Is Coming*. (Chicago: Fleming H. Revell Co., 1908).

14. Tim LaHaye. *Rapture Under Attack*. 142–145

15. John Walvoord. *The Rapture Question*. (Grand Rapides: Zondervan Publishing, 1979).

16. Tim LaHaye. *Rapture Under Attack*. 75–80.

17. Ibid., 75–80

18. Ibid., 180, 194, 228.

19. Ibid., 53, 75.

20. Ibid., 45, 180.

21. Ibid., 45.

22. Jimmy Evans. *Tipping Point: The End Is Here*. (Dallas: XO Publishing, 2020). 221–223.

23. Ibid., 213–216.

BIBLIOGRAPHY

_____. *Ante-Nicene Fathers, Vol. 1.* Translated by Alexander Roberts and William Rambaut, edited by Alexander Roberts and James Donaldson, Buffalo: Christian Literature Publishing Co., 1885. https://www.newadvent.org/fathers/0103519.htm

Berry, George Ricker. *The Interlinear Greek-English New Testament With Lexicon and Synonyms.* Grand Rapids: Zondervan, 1980.

Blackstone. William. *Jesus Is Coming,* Chicago: Fleming H. Revell, 1908.

_____. *The Broadman Bible Commentary: Vol. 12, General Articles Hebrews-Revelation,* edited by Clifton Allen, John Durham, Roy Hunnicutt, Jr., John MacGorman, Frank Stagg, William Fallis, Joseph Green, and Howard Colson. Nashville: Broadman, 1972

Bullinger, E.W. *Figures of Speech Used in the Bible.* Grand Rapids: Baker Book House, 1968

Chafer, Lewis Sperry. *Systematic Theology, Volumes 5 and 6.* Grand Rapides: Kregel, 1948.

Collins English Dictionary – Complete & Unabridged 2012 Digital Edition, : William Collins Sons & Co., LTD. 1979, 1986 © Harper Collins, 2012.

Dickens, Charles. *A Tale of Two Cities,* edited by Richard Maxwell. London: Penguin Classics (2003) ISBN 978-0-14-143960-0

E.R Sandeen. *The Roots of Fundamentalism 1800-1930,* Chicago: Univ. of Chicago Press, 1970.

Evans, Jimmy. *Tipping Point: The End Is Here,* Dallas: XO Publishing, 2020.

Graham Cooke, *Pastoring People Prophetically*, (Pasadena: Santa Barbara 2009), Compact Disc

Irenaus. *Against Heresies, Book V, Chapters 19-31.* https://media-cloud.sermonaudio.com/text/6261891307.pdf.

John, Damien. *The Last Trump*, https://the-wise-shall-understand.com/the-last-trump/
    accessed last Dec. 2021.

Josephus. *The Works of Josephus: New Updated Edition*, translated by William Whiston. Peabody: Hendrickson, 1987.

Keener, Craig S. *Miracles: The Credibility of the New Testament Accounts, Vol. 1*, Grand Rapids: Baker, 2011.

LaHaye, Tim. *Rapture Under Attack*. Sisters: Multnomah, Inc., 1998.

Lindsey, Hal. *The Late Great Planet Earth*. Grand Rapides: Zondervan, 1977.

Marrs, Texe. *Millenium: Peace, Promises, and the Day They Take Our Money Away*, Austin: Living Truth, 1990.

Norman, Larry. *'I Wish We'd All Been Ready'*, with Fishmarket Combo, produced by Hal Yoergler. (Capitol Records, 1969).

Orwell, George. *1984*. New York: Harper Collins, 1949.

"Rosh HaShananh — The Feast of Trumpets". Accessed December 13, 2021. https://promisestoisrael.org/jewish-culture-2/jewish-holidays/rosh-hashanah-the-feast-of-trumpets/

Sarin, Vic, director. *Left Behind*. Canada; Namesake Entertainment, 2000. 1:40.

Slick, Matt. "Irenaus Against Heresies, Book 5, Chapters 19-31." Carm.org. July 2010. Early Church Fathers. https://

carm.org/irenaus-against-heresies-book-5-chapters-19-31-virgin/

Sloan, Robert B. *The People of God: Essays on the Believers Church*, edited by Paul Basden and David S.Dockery, 148-165, Nashville: Broadman, 1991.

Strong, James. *Strong's Exhaustive Concordance of the Bible*. Iowa Falls: Riverside Book and Bible House, 1951.

Switzer, John. "Do Catholics Believe In The Rapture". (Vol.79, No.8, 46), Aug. 2014.

https://uscatholic.org/articles/201408/do-catgholics-believe-in-the-rapture/ accessed Feb. 2022.

Thompson, Donald, director. *A Thief In The Night*. Directed by Donald Thompson. Iowa, United States; Mark IV Pictures, 1972. 1:09.

Tolbert, Malcolm O. *Layman's Bible Book Commentary*. Nashville: Broadman, 1980.

Walvoord, John. *The Rapture Question*, Grand Rapides: Zondervan, 1979.

Weinland, Ronald. *2008 God's Final Witness*. Cincinnati: the-end.com, inc., 2006.

Wachowski(s) Lana and Lilly, directors. *The Matrix*. United States and Australia; Warner Bros./Village Roadshow Pictures/Groucho Film Partnership, 1999. 2:16.

Western Asceticism, Volume XII, edited by Owen Chadwick et al. Philadelphia: Westminster, 1958.

"What Is the Feast of Trumpets". October 6, 2020. https://www.biblestudytools.com/bible-study/topical-studies/what-is-the-feast-of-trumpets.html

Williams, J. Rodman. *Renewal Theology: Salvation, the Holy Spirit and Christian Living*, Grand Rapids: Zondervan, 1990.

_____.The Pre-Trib Research Center. "Two Academical Exercises on Subjects Bearing the Following Titles, Millennium and Last Novelties". 17–28. https://www.pre-trib.org/articles/rev-morgan-edwards/message/two-academical-exercises-on-subjects-bearing-the-following-titles-millennium-last-novelties/read

Zemekis, Robert, director. *Back to the Future II*. Amblin Entertainment and Universal Pictures, 1989.1:48.